EQUALITY ISSUES FOR THE NEW MILLENNIUM

Equality Issues for the New Millennium

Edited by
SNEH SHAH

LONDON AND NEW YORK

First published 2000 by Ashgate Publishing

Reissued 2018 by Routledge
2 Park Square, Milton Park, Abingdon, Oxon, OX14 4RN
711 Third Avenue, New York, NY 10017, USA

Routledge is an imprint of the Taylor & Francis Group, an informa business

Copyright © Sneh Shah 2000

All rights reserved. No part of this book may be reprinted or reproduced or utilised in any form or by any electronic, mechanical, or other means, now known or hereafter invented, including photocopying and recording, or in any information storage or retrieval system, without permission in writing from the publishers.

Notice:
Product or corporate names may be trademarks or registered trademarks, and are used only for identification and explanation without intent to infringe.

Publisher's Note
The publisher has gone to great lengths to ensure the quality of this reprint but points out that some imperfections in the original copies may be apparent.

Disclaimer
The publisher has made every effort to trace copyright holders and welcomes correspondence from those they have been unable to contact.

A Library of Congress record exists under LC control number: 132586

ISBN 13: 978-1-138-32835-8 (hbk)
ISBN 13: 978-1-138-32836-5 (pbk)
ISBN 13: 978-0-429-44870-6 (ebk)

Contents

List of Figures and Tables   *vii*
List of Contributors   *viii*
Foreword by Norman Thomas   *xii*

1   Introduction: Where from? Where to?   1
    Sneh Shah

2   Single Issues to Coherent Campaign: Pitfalls and Possibilities   13
    Robin Grinter

3   Gender and Race: Maintaining and Crossing Boundaries   24
    Sneh Shah

4   Asian Women Undergraduates and their Attitudes to British Schooling: A Complex Issue   33
    Harkirtan Singh-Raud

5   Sins of Omission: Teacher Education and Race   46
    Russell Jones

6   The Reality of Isolation for Black Student Teachers   62
    Sue Lewis

7   Male Students on Primary Initial Teacher Education Courses   73
    Mary Thornton

8   A New Millennium for Disabled Students in Higher Education?   89
    Lea Myers and Viv Parker

9	Enhancing Opportunities for Disabled Students: Comparisons across the Atlantic *Miranda Preston and Jennie Gorbold*	103
10	The Role of the Student Counselling Service in the Promotion of Equal Opportunities in Education in the New Millennium *Ruth Caleb and Heidi Gilhooly*	111
11	Is Bilingualism an Obstacle to Inclusion for Deaf Children? *Joy Jarvis*	121
12	Responding Locally to Global Inequality *Peter Bloomfield*	131
13	Democracy and Education *Séan Stitt*	142
14	Conclusion *Sneh Shah*	157

Index *161*

List of Figures and Tables

Figures

12.1　An Example of LA 21　　　　　　　　　　　139

Tables

4.1　Significance of mother tongue teaching　　　　38

4.2　Asian topics in schools　　　　　　　　　　　40

7.1　Gender inequality in teaching positions　　　　76

7.2　Gender analysis of ITE cohorts　　　　　　　78

13.1　Student teachers' views on human rights education　　155

List of Contributors

Peter Bloomfield, BSc, PGCE, MA; Senior Lecturer in Geography and Education at the University of Hertfordshire. His subjects are Geography, Primary Geographical Education and Environmental Education. He is a member of the Geographical Association's Primary and Middle School Committee and of the St Albans 'Agenda 21 Forum' Steering Group.

Ruth Caleb, BSc, Diploma in Counselling, MA in Counselling and Psychotherapy; currently Senior Student Counsellor at Thames Valley University, she is a UKCP registered psychotherapist in private practice. She also teaches on the MSc Therapeutic Counselling at Greenwich University. She has eight years' experience in University Student Counselling, and over seventeen years' experience as a counsellor in a variety of settings including agencies dealing with drug abuse, HIV and AIDS, pregnancy and abortion, and with children and young people.

Heidi Gilhooly, BSc, RMN, Diploma in Counselling, MA in Counselling; originating from Finland, she currently works as a College Counsellor in a Further Education establishment and as a Staff Counsellor for the National Health Service. She is BAC accredited and has fourteen years' experience as a counsellor in a variety of settings, including agencies dealing with mental health, drug abuse and HIV, and during the last four years, in universities and colleges.

Jennie Gorbold is a Special Needs Co-ordinator at The Chichester Institute of Higher Education. She was a member of a regional consortium funded by the Higher Education Funding Council for England to develop work on disability issues in higher education. Although she trained to teach children and adults with dyslexia, she has spent time in Israel with Reuven Feuerstein, being trained in instrumental enrichment.

Robin Grinter is Director of the Centre for Education for Equality at Didsbury School of Education, Manchester Metropolitan University. The Centre was set up in 1995 to integrate all aspects of work in teacher education for equality and social justice. Much of his work has been directed towards promoting multicultural, antiracist and equality education in the curriculum. He taught history for ten years in comprehensive schools in Cheshire and Sheffield, and has been a Senior Lecturer in the Arts and Humanities Department of the Didsbury School of Education since 1971. He has published numerous articles and chapters in books exploring the relationship between multicultural and antiracist education, and the opportunities for implementing these and other equality issues through the National Curriculum. He is also a member of the Antiracist Teacher Education Network.

Joy Jarvis is a teacher of the deaf and is currently responsible for training teachers of the deaf at the University of Hertfordshire. She has worked in a range of contexts with deaf children and adults. This has included working with families of deaf children and as an advisory teacher in schools and colleges. Her current research is about issues surrounding children's access to classroom language, particularly the language used by the teacher and areas of potential in relation to the needs of children with linguistic delay or difference.

Russell Jones lectures in English at John Moores University, Liverpool. He worked for seven years with British Rail and acted as Trade Union representative. He completed a degree in English and spent eight years working in primary schools in Cheshire and North Staffordshire. He has taught art at Keele University and history at Manchester Metropolitan University. He completed his doctorate as a full-time student, the focus of the research being student teacher education in exclusive white contexts. That has since been published as a book with the title, 'Teaching Racism- or Tackling it?: Multicultural Stories from White Beginning Teachers'.

Sue Lewis gained a BA in English from King's College, London, and an MA in Education from the Open University. She taught English, Drama and English for Speakers of Other Languages in Sweden, London and North Wales. In 1989 she was appointed Equal Opportunities Co-ordinator for Clwyd Education Authority and became the Welsh representative to the European Women's Lobby in Brussels. Since 1993 she has been a Senior Lecturer in Secondary Education at the Crewe and Alsaber Faculty, Manchester Metropolitan University.

Lea Myers is a lecturer in Special Educational Needs at the University of East London, Department of Education and Community Studies.

Viv Parker is Reader in Educational Development and Co-ordinator for Students with Disabilities at the University of East London which has successfully bid at each of the three phases of funding from HEFCE.

Miranda Preston is Senior lecturer in Special Educational Needs at The Chichester Institute of Higher Education. She has worked in schools in the United States of America, France and Britain for over twenty years. She writes on a variety of special needs topics and works on a consultative basis for several special needs advisory groups. Her publications include 'Four Times Harder: Six Case Studies of Students with Dyslexia in Higher Education'.

Sneh Shah BA, MA, PGCE, PGCE, FRSA; is the Director of the Centre for Equality Issues in Education, University of Hertfordshire. The Centre was set up in 1995 and its activities include annual conferences and establishing links with local, national and international organisations. She is also the Editor of New Era in Education, published three times a year by World Education Fellowship. Her recent research projects have included an evaluation of the Pilot Project for the Mentoring Project funded by World Studies Trust, and the project on Access Course students becoming qualified teachers was funded by the Teacher Training Agency.

Harkirtan Singh-Raud PhD is a Senior Lecturer with the Department of Education and Community Studies at John Moores University, Liverpool.

Séan Stitt BA, PhD, Diploma in Social Work, is currently with St Martin's College, Lancaster University. He was a Community Worker in Belfast for seven years, Lecturer in Social Policy at Newcastle upon Tyne Polytechnic, Reader in Community Studies at John Moores University, Liverpool, and Director of Research at National College for Industrial Relations, Dublin. His publications include 'Poverty: Rowntree Visited', 'Poverty and Poor Relief: Concepts and Reality' and 'Poverty and Rowntree 4'.

Norman Thomas taught in primary schools in London and Hertfordshire, finally as a headteacher. He joined the HM Inspectorate of Schools (England) in 1962 and retired as Chief Inspector of Primary and Middle Schools in 1981. He chaired a Committee of Inquiry in

Inner London in 1985; the report of which, entitled 'Improving Primary Education' was published by Inner London Education Authority. He acted as a Specialist Advisor to the House of Commons Education Select Committee between 1984 and 1997. In the past he has been a Visiting Professor of Education at the Polytechnic of East London, an Honorary Professor at Warwick University, a Specialist Professor of Primary Education at Nottingham University and is currently Visiting Professor with the University of Hertfordshire. As a writer he has contributed numerous chapters in books on education and articles in professional journals. His book, 'Primary Education from Plowden to the 1990s', was published in 1990.

Mary Thornton is Education Research Leader and a Principal Lecturer in the Department of Education at the University of Hertfordshire. Formerly a primary teacher in the London Borough of Brent, she has taught across a wide range of undergraduate and post-graduate initial teacher education and continued professional development courses, and non-teacher education and sociology courses. She has externally examined primary initial teacher education and continued professional development courses in other institutions. Her current research interests lie in the areas of gender inequality, primary teaching and the primary curriculum.

Foreword

NORMAN THOMAS

The chapters included in this volume relate to issues of equality in the treatment of individuals. The titles show the wide range of issues covered and the texts reveal at least some of the complexities. Some of the authors acknowledge and take pleasure in progress that has been made in improving fairness in the treatment of individuals and groups. All identify more that should and must be done. The specific references to authors made in this foreword do justice to none of them.

The complexity and the range of concerns derive from two sources: one is the unique blend of characteristics that form each person; and the other the seemingly endless number of characteristics, singly and in combination, that lead people to recognise their membership of one or another community. The community may be world-wide and in no sense a minority, for example, female/feminine as distinct from male/masculine and, as we are shown by Mary Thornton have implications for the ways in which individuals are encouraged to make the best of their talents both for themselves and for the general good. Indeed, Peter Bloomfield, warning us about the judicious use of resources and reminding us that we 'borrow the earth from our children', puts the whole of today's world population into a group distinct from but obliged to act fairly towards its successors.

On the other hand, Harkirtan Singh-Raud is concerned with the position of what are, in England, minority groups - Sikh, Hindu and Muslim women undergraduates - and is determined that they should not be lumped mistakenly together as 'Asian', and their differences unrecognised and unmet. Of course, they are members of families whose recent ancestors lived in Asia, but they have distinct cultural and religious traditions and beliefs that may affect their daily lives differently, for example, in their inclination to enter a university away from their home area. The traditions of their community also affect them differently because they are women and not men, so that there is a double distinction, neither part of which is wholly consistent across groups. Add to that the individual and family differences within each group and sub-group, and the dangers inherent in stereotyping mount. As Russell Jones and Sue Lewis indicate, the danger may be all the greater where people with little or no experience of minority groups are either all too ready to express opinions about them or presume that there is no distinction to be made: the invidious danger of 'colour-blindness'.

Physical, sensory and mental disabilities occur in individuals in all parts of the world and without respect to class, colour, culture, race or religion, though maybe in different proportions. The individuals concerned may find it more rather than less difficult than others to establish membership of a community and lose the advantages that comradeship can bring. Joy Jarvis highlights a particular aspect of that with regard to the profoundly deaf, and challenges the simplistic view that provision should be aimed only at securing the individual's place in the mainstream may, in this case undervaluing sign language, fall short of what is necessary. Miranda Preston and Jennie Gorbold raise different issues that might be seen as the obverse of that.

To what extent and in what ways is it legitimate to make unusual provision so that the special needs of individuals are met, both during education/training and subsequently in work? Provision has improved, though practice varies more than principle, and reliable information is hard to come by. All the more reason, then, to pay attention to Lea Myers' and Viv Parker's contribution, and to think carefully about the implications of what Ruth Caleb and Heidi Gilhooly have to say about student counselling. Counselling has a vital part to play before entry to higher education, during it, and before employment. Learning about oneself is as important a part of the educational process as is learning about the world at large.

Through all of these chapters run questions about who is responsible and for what. Seán Stitt prefers to leave decisions about moral values to individual parents and teachers rather than to governments, and he and others regard the National Curriculum as failing to draw children's and teachers' attention sufficiently to issues of race, culture, religion and class. However, some requirements for specific provision are likely to be beyond the scope of individuals or single families, and Robin Grinter's argument is persuasive that there are also advantages in conducting a coherent campaign, combining aspects of specific issues, and aimed at providing for 'non-standard' circumstances.

Whether policies are formed and action is taken by individuals, institutions or government, they need to be informed by reliable evidence, and Sneh Shah's leadership of the Conference that stimulated the production of this book provides an important contribution to that knowledge. All in all we should be pleased progress is being made in the difficult matter of treating people fairly, which sometimes turns out to mean differently, and be encouraged to greater effort. Perhaps, at the core, is the requirement that we respond to and support people as they actually are, and that we do not jump to conclusions, and worse, to action, because one aspect or another of their personality, behaviour, beliefs or looks is, in our terms, non-standard. After all, that very same oddity must seem to them to be evidence of a peculiarity in us. Whichever way round you look at it.

1 Introduction: Where from? Where to?

SNEH SHAH

Location of Equality Issues

A key concern as we enter the New Millennium is the location of equality issues. When the word equality is mentioned different people tend to go for different meanings, highlighting the many and varied assumptions that we have about equality. A common conclusion is that it is something to do with feminist issues, or if the context is cultural diversity, then the concern must be to do with minority ethnic communities. Sometimes issues of gender, race and class are put together, but generally extensive care needs to be taken to understand the context and the meaning of the term.

It is unfortunate that the details around equality are being pushed into such narrow channels, and in such a way that marginalisation continues. A pertinent question, therefore is what is the differences between equality as a theme in Britain after the Second World War when issues of egalitarianism were important, and Britain in the late 1990s? Or between 1960s, when there was a lot of dialogue in academic/professional education fields about education as an agent of change, and 1990s where equality is being talked about in a patchy fashion and sometimes quite superficially? And what is the future?

Key Features Around the 1970s

It is quite useful to take the 1970s as a focus period. Two pieces of legislation dealing with aspects of equality in the United Kingdom were passed then: The Sex Discrimination (1975) and The Race Relations (1976) Acts. The legislation on race was a major achievement. The Sex Discrimination Act echoed very clearly the focus on equal pay for equal work between men and women. The links between the legislation and education in practice were very tenuous. Changes in the latter were affected to a certain extent by the thinking behind the legislation, but generally took place independently. The race relations dialogues, anticipating the recommendation of the (Great Britain, 1981) Rampton Report, started looking at structural and societal issues. Parallel to that, the deficit model highlighting the exotic nature of the minority ethnic cultures led to a tokenistic approach in classroom practice. Tokenism was widespread, although the overall take up of the issues generally was limited to schools, and in a patchy fashion. Sex discrimination issues primarily focused on raising the achievement of girls and getting them to take up subjects normally dominated by boys.

Much heated debate focused on what was the ideal model for society. An assimilationalist stance was at one end and an integrationist one at another, with focus on others such as a pluralistic one. Home Office funding of projects, under Section 11 of the Local Government Act (1966), to support children from families from the New Commonwealth and Pakistan, was on the one hand welcomed by Local Education Authorities (LEA) and parents who felt there were specific needs of bilingual children that required additional resources. A very strong lobby, on the other hand, opposed that on the premise that it was promoting a deficit model based on the notion of a racial hierarchy, echoing an imperialistic, racial framework.

Special needs was highlighted by Bernard Coard in his book (1971) indicating how black children were being disadvantaged by the system and wrongly classified as educationally sub-normal. Apart from this, special needs, under the different labels such as Educationally Sub-Normal (ESN), was not seen as clearly as an equality issue. The Warnock Report's findings were significant for schools, but seen in a different category.

Europe featured in some respects. Those concerned about bilingualism tried, with limited success, to use the European Commission guidelines on language needs for children of migrant workers to get local and national governments to take action. Some of the literature on gender issues referred to policy and practice in Europe but the active impact of European developments on Britain was limited.

Key Features of the 1990s

Much of the progress made in both race relations and sex equality issues was over-shadowed in the late 1980s and 1990s by what were deemed to be more important national matters such as raising national standards in reading and writing. Some legislation, especially in relation to sex discrimination, was aimed at responding to gaps identified in the 1975 legislation. Perhaps the key feature in this period was the beginning of some real impact of developments and policies in Europe, although still in a patchy fashion. European funding, for instance from the European Social Fund, gave a boost to many projects on specific or general minority group needs, equality between men and women, and action for socially excluded groups.

Discussion of racism in the European Parliament, and specific initiatives such as 1997, European Year Against Racism encouraged further activity in many ways such as by Local Authorities and in the field of the education of young people. At a national level in Britain, discussions on the amendments necessary to the 1976 Race Relations Act have been taking place. Another major achievement was the Protection from Harassment Act 1997, enabling victims of harassment to claim damages, apply for a civil injunction to prevent it continuing, or even prosecute through the criminal courts. Perhaps the most important, development however, was The Disability Discrimination Act (1995). The National Disability Council was set up as an independent statutory Society to advise on issues and implementation of the Act. Thus in many respects a pattern similar to that for racial and sexual discrimination was set up - Acts followed by the setting up of the Equal Opportunities Commission and the Commission for Racial Equality.

At the level of schools, the Education Reform Act (1988) in some ways put equality into practice, for instance, by making subjects such as science and technology compulsory for boys and girls; yet it was also discriminatory as the curriculum requirements did not apply to independent schools. The initial emphasis on equal opportunities (referring to boys and girls) and multiculturalism disappeared with the revisions of the National Curriculum. Overall, the new curriculum for schools reflected an assimilationist model, as epitomised by Religious Education.

As a part of the basic curriculum, religious education focused on Christianity. Nick Tate, when he was the Chief Executive of the School Curriculum and Assessment Authority, expressed very clearly the rationale behind the content. He gave a number of reasons. One was that (SCAA 1997, p.12):

> A fundamental purpose of the school curriculum is to transmit an appreciation of, and commitment to, the best of the culture we have inherited. Education is not simply about introducing pupils to an array of cultural delights and leaving them to make their own cultural and moral choices. This would reinforce our current sense of rootlessness and confusion of identity.

His second point was that the cultural dimension of the curriculum needed to be firmly rooted in Greece and Rome, in Christianity and traditions of European civilisation. Thus the curriculum emphasised the centrality of British history, English literary heritage, and study of Christianity.

Finally, Tate believed that we should recognise that in our society the best guarantee of minority cultures was a strong majority culture that valued itself, and signalled that tradition and cultures were worthy of respect.

Attempts by black groups and educationalists from all backgrounds who supported such policies, i.e. accepting the rights of the different cultural groups and asking for social justice, were presented as a sign of the failure of the minority groups to assimilate to what was regarded as true British society, and not as a sign of discrimination by the British society. They were portrayed as asking for special privileges and were causing a threat to the traditions and culture of British society (Dijk, 1988).

The view expressed by Rob Philips, giving a Welsh perspective (SCAA, 1997), can be a pointer to a harmonious future. He highlighted that nations are not natural entities but are manufactured, like national identity. He also went on to say that (SCAA, 1997) 'effective citizenship requires tolerance and, understanding of the other'. In his view there was the need for an education system which produced citizens with a properly informed perception of their own identity as well as that of others. It should, amongst others, also promote an inclusivist view of community, society and nation, and address the universal rather than the particular.

Separately, because of the pressure from teachers, LEAs and parents, the Home Office funding of Section 11 projects continued, albeit reduced and for a short time only, and gradually to be the responsibility of the Department for Education and Employment. The Swann Report (Great Britain, 1985), following the Rampton Report of 1981, had led to new policies and change, although still patchy, of practice in many schools, further education colleges, and teacher education institutions. However, the pressure of a prescriptive curriculum for schools had an obvious impact on the training institutions. The changes in the structure of the policy making institutions, such as the creation of Teacher Training Agency, the separation of further and higher education institutions from LEAs, and Local Management of Schools additionally meant equality issues were not generally central to the functioning of the individual institutions.

Generally, the legislation currently in force has had a limited effect on making the further and higher education institutions in particular take issues of equality seriously. Two guides (Commission for Racial Equality et al. 1996; 1997) clearly set out agendas and plans of action for further and higher education institutions, but they are not mandatory.

The Challenges for the New Millennium

As we enter the new millennium, it is critical that we take stock of where we are in relation to equality, what are some of the tensions and conflicts, and how we should aim to move forward.

Parameters of Equality

There have been different philosophies underpinning these movements. Some have been event/subject specific, some have been based on egalitarian ideas and others on ideas of social justice or equality. Applications of philosophy have also been varied.

In this context the term equality has been used widely but with different meanings. Often terms have been used as if they are interchangeable, although that should only happen if the true meanings of the different terms were understood. What should be included? Issues of gender and culture have been generally accepted, but with race, it is inconsistent. Special needs is sometimes treated separately from equality issues, although logically this cannot be justified.

Lack of a critical overview generally leads to individuals and organisations working passionately to support their own area of concern. The result is that scarce resources are divided, and experiences in one area do not benefit others. Some attempts have been made to bring issues of race and gender in non-British and global dialogues but the effectiveness of academic and professional movements in the British context is limited.

Taking the common narrow channelling of equality issues, it is evident that there is concern about equality in a wider range of fields. The word equality begins to raise a whole range of philosophical as well as practical concerns, and academic/professional issues. Lessons learnt from race equality debates, for instance, need to be applied to concerns about the environment. The conference at the Centre for Equality Issues in Education, University of Hertfordshire, held in November 1997, provided a critical forum. The call for papers was open and the response came from a wide range of interests. This was crucial because in the second half of the twentieth century in Britain has seen a gradual but definite erosion of the space for dialogue and advancement of thought. There is an urgent need to retrieve this which has been lost because of the application of a market force economy to higher education.

End of Ghettoisation

One of the most critical targets has to be an end to the continued categorisation of issues. Debates in the 1970s had included a discussion of this within the field of racial concerns and education. However, protagonists of positive policy to combat racial discrimination and promote cultural harmony had strongly objected to having issues of gender and class brought into their arguments. Their position was very clear that the significance of racial/cultural issues was properly understood before it was saddled up with others, however important those themes might be. There was also the belief that the people who proposed an alliance were more interested in lowering the significance of these issues; it was almost as if they had found a subtle, but unchallengeable way of opposing real change.

Since then there has been some weakening of the boundaries. This has arisen partly because within the minority ethnic communities there has been an increasing focus on the impacting on their lives of gender and class issues. Much of the writing of black women is evidence of their need to focus on how they had been affected by sexism, from black as well as white men. There is also concern within many white feminist organisations that feminism has often been racist and while claims of solidarity have been made, they have been on the terms of white women. Links between special needs and racism had been established as long ago as the 1970s when Bernard Coard published his seminal work on the West Indian child being made educationally sub-normal within the British education system. There have been other significant studies in relation to such inter-relationships, highlighting the double disadvantage that is being suffered by many people.

The frameworks of the conferences organised by Centre for Equality Issues in Education, University of Hertfordshire, deliberately avoided specific, separate, categories for issues such as gender, race, culture, class, and special needs. The presentations were evidence of many educationalists' desire to see equality incoporating but going beyond these aspects, and the way they were currently seen and presented in the institutions.

What are the possible reasons for this continued narrow definition of equality, and of continued ghettoisation into the individual areas of equality? The tradition, perhaps deliberate, of seeing equal opportunities as related to gender, of separating special needs as in the context of the National Curriculum, and in relation to students in further and higher education, has continued. It could be argued that the issues are so complex that it is an inevitable reaction that they are seen and handled separately. The strong academic tradition of specialising and the assumed need to specify subjects has put in jeopardy individuals and studies that prioritise a holistic approach. It is also possible that many individuals find it difficult to handle racism and use other equality issues as evidence of their liberalism.

From the Periphery to the Centre

There are current discussions about mainstreaming in the context of the Equal Opportunities Commission and the Commission for Racial Equality, although this is concern that the specificity of each separate 'cause' may get watered down with mainstreaming. Pressure on policy making bodies can be greater if there is unity on the part of the campaigners. While the identified cause may be unique, underlying causes and processes to change in attitudes have a lot in common.

Mainstreaming, however, needs to be more than an inclusion of race, gender and special needs in any discussion or decision. For there to be fundamental changes in attitudes and practice, the focal point throughout has to be equality. The education of all teachers for the future should have these issues included without them being singled out. Commitment of policy is imperative in order to avoid the 'permeation' of the 1980s, which in reality was an excuse to do very little.

A very important adjunct is the encouragement and space for an open dialogue. There are many assumptions about both the context of any seminars/conferences about a specific aspect of equality, and who is expected to attend. At a recent conference on gender perspectives, out of around sixty participants, there were three males: one was an invited speaker, one was a workshop leader and the third was the partner/driver of another speaker. When asked, other male colleagues stated that they kept away as they assumed a conference on gender was for female participants only.

What should be included? The current discussions around the terms and contexts of 'inclusion' and 'exclusion' raise two key areas for action. The first one is a decision about what should be included. This leads to a questioning of the validity of the different terms. For instance, is there any reason why bilingualism should be restricted to spoken languages only?

The vitality of the educationists' theorising about the role of education needs to be restored in the new millennium so that the questions that a concern for equality raises become catalysts for a serious re-think about education, as was the case in the 1980s.

Equality and Quality

Quality is currently significant in education in Britain. Funding and status are very much linked to judgements about quality. An overview of equality issues in education is likely to give a very patchy, almost peripheral picture when assessments in quality are made. This generally indicates equality has not been analysed and accepted as a key factor in quality maintenance and assessment. However, there is some movement towards an increasing emphasis on equality.

Definitions of quality are varied; some believe the concept is an impossible one to deal with abstractly. There is no agreement about the exact meaning of quality and its application. It could refer to very high standards, consistency (or zero defects), fitness for purpose, or value for money. The danger, according to Conrad (1994), is that the reasons for working with such a concept are rarely questioned and the concept itself is seldom defined. Thus there could, in reality, be one of many diverse interpretations of the word quality, as applied to a specific institution. The more common applications of quality relate to higher education institutions as business enterprises. It can be taken as consistency, or it can be measured in terms of the end product, i.e. the level and percentage of student passes. It could be value for money, or it could be high standards. Then again the question would be, who defines those standards?

There are, however, other possibilities. Nightingale and O'Neil (1994) indicate a preference for equality because it is transformative and it empowers students. The purpose of university education then would be to develop the general qualities of a personal and social as well as those of an intellectual kind. Outcomes would relate to inter-personal skills, communication, problem-solving abilities, planning and strategic thinking abilities, and others.

With reference to schools, Frith and Mahoney believe that (1994, p.1-2):

> what many have failed to realise is that quality and equality are inextricably linked. How can we attempt to raise standards through the delivery of a new curriculum and with new methods of assessment, without using the knowledge we have gained about the different effect of teaching style and grouping on pupil performance?

Thus any school, which is not looking at issues of equality, is bound to fail.

So equality is not a very straightforward concept that refers to a single aspect such as the number of minority ethnic students. If applied comprehensively, it gets the institutions to question a whole range of issues which are related to their prime purpose. As stated by Ouseley and Bahl (Commission for Racial Equality, 1996), good equal opportunities practice can improve the quality of service in all areas of teaching and learning.

The question that thus needs to be posed is what are the possible reasons why the narrower definitions of quality, which are based more on business premises are in application, with little attention paid to equality?

Individual Versus the Group

Each person is a unique blend of characteristics. It is normally the case that the seemingly endless number of characteristics, individually and in combination, lead people to recognise their membership of one or other community.

Academic and professional responses to these two aspects have, sometimes with justification, been varied. The variations have focused on one aspect of people's characteristics and the implications of membership of that category. Which characteristics have been focused on has depended on a range of factors such as the strength of beliefs of certain individuals who have been able to influence many people, who wield power, desire to resolve conflict, and have the political aim to achieve some kind of equilibrium in society.

Human beings are complex creatures like the organisations that they live in. To a certain extent this has been accepted in education when it is acknowledged that any individual may have multiple identities. However, grouping of people continues. It is often argued that in order to demonstrate disadvantage, monitoring of people in specific categories needs to take place. Reasons for not taking any action from those that are opposed to promoting equality include lack of evidence, research, or statistics. The dilemma that is posed is that continued categorisation perpetuates a range of labels are used and the users do not have the understanding to locate a particular label in the overall context of equality.

Equality and Research

There is general awareness of the potential and problems with research in specific areas of equality. One example is the significance of the influence of the researcher's background on the framework and results of the research; it is likely that a male researcher may not be able to empathise as much with the issues of gender equality especially if the subjects are female. Similarly, black researchers are more likely to understand the context of the experiences of black subjects. White researchers may be conditioned by imperial and neo-imperial ideologies and their research findings could confirm existing stereotypes.

Sound research in any case should be the goal of any thorough researcher. Rather than limiting the conduct of the research to certain groups of researchers, who by way of their background are deemed to be the appropriate researchers, the whole process of training researchers and of examining the work of researchers needs to be updated (Shah, 1998). Awareness of equality issues for all researchers will ensure there will be more thought, all-embracing dialogue, and better application.

The Wider Context of Formal Education

Recent changes in education in the United Kingdom have included judgements on quality of the education funded on the basis of the employment record of the newly qualified. Institutions of higher education have increasingly made links with employers as a key target, exemplified in the type of education to be funded. Connections with the world of employment, however, are complex. Employment on its own, while important, can be a narrow focus for the education providers. There are a range of issues such as the adequacy of the provision in relation to the employment market, and of the mechanism of catering for the needs of each insdidual student. A match between the ethos of the higher education institution and that of the employing organisations is also imperative.

As is clear from the rising number of permanent exclusions from schools, an education institution which is going to be judged on success for its quality, may try hard to either not accept, or somehow ease the departure of those that may seem to need special, extra attention. Hence there are many questions that education providers have to face in the new millennium, such as the strength and commitment of their stated mission to the range of issues that enable students with a range of

The Focus of this Book

The book is raising challenges which educators have to take up in order that the beginning of the new millennium is not just a regurgitation of the dialogues of this century but a move forward. The discreet and the underlying focus of the chapters is an attempt to take a fresh look at the definition of equality and how education can interpret and implement it. It is clear that we need to cut across, bring together, and find links between the themes that have been particularly detailed recently in the United Kingdom, so that the term equality is seen in as broad a framework as possible. Some of the 'traditional areas' are examined but the relevance of others has to be detailed and justified.

Bringing equality issues to the centre is essential for good educational reasons. At the same time specific areas such as race need to be focused on. Hence the chapters include a detailed analysis of recent developments with indications of what specific policy and practical developments are essential.

Moving forward means paying more attention to the complexities of labelling. There are no clear answers but theory, research and practice have to be involved in an ongoing dialogue to avoid going from the disadvantages of one set of labels to another. With the Department for Education and Science in Britain changing to the Department for Education and Employment, there is a real necessity and urgency of linking education to employment in a broader context than that of graduates getting jobs.

Very serious comprehensive dialogues, however, have to precede changes but can be effective.

Bibliography

Blackstone, T., Parekh, B. and Sanders, P.(eds) (1998), *Race Relations in Britain: A Developing Agenda*, Routledge, London.
Coard, B. (1971), *How the West Indian Child is made Educationally Sub-normal in the British School System*, New Beacon Books, London.
Commission for Racial Equality and Equal Opportunities Commission (1996), *Further Education and Equality: A Managers Manual*, CRE and EOC, London.
Commission for Racial Equality (1996), *Roots of the Future: Ethnic Diversity in the Making of Britain*, Commission for Racial Equality, London.
Conrad, J. (1994), *A Discussion of the Concept of Quality in Relation to Educational Planning, Taking Nepal as an Example*, Paper presented at the conference, Quality of Education in the Context of Culture in Developing Countries, Tampere, Finland.
Dijk, T. van (1988), *New Analysis: Case Studies of International and National News in the Press*, Lawrence Erlbaum, New Jersey, USA.

Great Britain, Department of Education and Science (1981), *The Education of West Indian Children*, HMSO, London.

Great Britain, Department of Education and Science (1985), *Education for All*, HMSO, London.

Frith, R. and Mahoney, P.(eds) (1994), *Promoting Quality and Equality in Schools: Empowering Teachers Through Change*, David Foulton, London.

Nightingale, P. and O'Neil, M. (1994), *Achieving Quality Learning in Higher Education*, Kogan Page, London.

Powney, J., Hamilton, S. and Weiner, G. (1997), *Higher Education and Equality: A Guide*, Equal Opportunities Commission, Commission for Racial Equality, and Committee of Vice-Chancellors and Principals of the Universities of the UK, London.

School Curriculum and Assessment Authority (1997), *Curriculum, Culture and Society*, SCAA, London.

Shah, S. (1998), 'Career Pathways and Minority Ethnic Researchers. Some Issues', in *New Era in Education*, vol. 79, pp. 70-75.

Shah, S. (ed) (1996), *National Initiatives and Equality Issues*, Centre for Equality Issues in Education, University of Hertfordshire, UK.

Shah, S. (ed) (1995), *Refugees and Asylum Seekers and Higher Education*, Centre for Equality Issues in Education, University of Hertfordshire, UK.

2 Single Issues to Coherent Campaign: Pitfalls and Possibilities

ROBIN GRINTER

Abstract

This chapter is an exploration of one of the definitive processes in the 1990s in the field of education for equality. Forward-looking practitioners have sought to draw together the separate campaigns for greater equality in education and Western societies in general. These campaigns include work for racial justice, gender equality, the reduction of impact of homophobia on gays and lesbians, the increasing of the life chances of those with disabilities and many others. There are implications of all the single issues, but class overrides them all. Attempts to draw together all these separate campaigns together in a concern to educate for equality have taken different forms. There are pitfalls, but more important are the links between the different issues. Underpinning the discussion is the need to understand not just the rhetoric of the term equality, but its potentially powerful value, if applied properly.

The chapter analyses the impact of poverty and the process of exclusion, and the role of education in inclusion and exclusion. It examines the potential conflict that exists between these different groups and how education for equality can bridge the gaps between them. What is being proposed should help to create a sensitivity to the complexity of experiences of children as members of their communities that may enable teachers to identify more closely with the reality of their pupils' needs, and to make even more significant contributions to helping them meet them effectively. In view of the rigid framework of the National Curriculum in Britain, it is crucial that teachers understand and apply the issues of equality to their teaching.

The Context of Free Market Politics and Social Inequality

This chapter is an exploration of one of the definitive processes in the 1990s in the field of education for equality. It is encapsulated in the titles of the Equality Centres at the Universities of Manchester Metropolitan and Hertfordshire: forward-looking practitioners have sought to draw together in teacher education the separate campaigns for greater equality in education and Western societies in general. These campaigns include all work for racial justice in the form of antiracist and multicultural education, and for gender equality through feminist and antisexist education. More specialised campaigns have focused on the need to reduce the impact of homophobia on gays and lesbians, and increase the life chances of those with disabilities. There are other significant campaigns, as many as there are groups of people who may be considered to have their life chances reduced through prejudice and devaluation; these include the elderly and the homeless in the wider society, and children whose educational opportunities are reduced or destroyed by the experience of being bullied or abused.

Attempts to draw all these separate campaigns together in a concern to educate for equality have taken different forms. These include education for equal opportunities for all, education that contributes to the creation of a more equal society, education to increase awareness of the nature and impact of separate forms of inequality, and education to nurture the determination and skills to reduce inequalities. Most Centres or campaigns have included several of these elements, woven together with different emphases. Their unifying theme is that they have all been the outcome of an increase in poverty and reduction of life chances which some may see as the result of government action informed by a philosophy based on a belief in the virtues of inequality, and the outcome of market policies which would unavoidably create increased inequality in society and economic life (Hattersley, 1995). In the wider and more political context, all concerned for education for equality have been part of the struggle to preserve some opportunities for the increasing number of people deprived of hope and ambition by their experience of poverty and unemployment. All the initiatives under examination were developments born in the experience of adversity.

The Impact of Poverty and the Process of Exclusion

This shared experience means that all Centres and campaigns for equality in education in Britain relate closely to issues of class, whether they focus on it or not. Increasing poverty has many effects on the experiences of pupils. This can be a direct impact - a reduction in the amount of time spent in schools because of ill health, lack of resources such as books, an absence of parental contact and support because of shift work, or lack of time for school work because of responsibilities to care for younger siblings.

Poverty has other indirect effects because it increases the impact of other forms of inequality, or at least has a significant influence on the way they operate. For example, many black pupils live in communities where they will experience the impact of poverty. Any resentment, assertiveness and alienation from schooling that results may well confirm some teachers in low expectations that derive from the stereotypes of racism, and add to the pressures on pupils In the worst scenario for black British pupils this leads to high levels of exclusion that almost inevitably mean a total denial of life chances (Gillborn and Gipps, 1996).

Gender issues can also be enhanced in the context of the educational experience of black British pupils, though not perhaps in the conventional way. Many black British boys, facing already limited prospects for employment in the inner city and knowing that these may well be made doubly worse by the long-established racism of potential employers (Smith, 1997), are likely to lack the motivation to achieve and find themselves ill-equipped to take up parental responsibilities. However the evidence shows that many black British girls face the challenge of the prospect of single parenting and full family responsibilities by determined efforts to succeed academically and increase their employability and earning power (Gillborn and Gipps, 1996).

The impact of class runs deeper still. All who have any concern for social equality are, of course, well aware that the nature of the education process in any society is fundamental to its quality. Schooling in any society is, after all, designed to promote its values and beliefs, and to prepare its children to fit into and maintain the particular structures of the society into which they have been born (Illich, 1971). British society is peculiarly unequal, because it is still deeply influenced by considerations of class, and the education system is designed to reinforce these. Not merely do we have public schools which provide unique opportunities for those with wealth and social cachet to dominate public life, but the British comprehensive system has always been weakened by opportunities for affluent parents to advance the interests of their already advantaged children. This can be done by taking their children out of the system and sending them to independent, grant maintained or grammar schools in areas like Trafford that still maintain the tripartite system. Others, with more limited resources, or with a residue of social concern, play the comprehensive system to their benefit by securing entry for their children to schools high in the class-distorted but deeply influential academic league tables.

It is equally significant for this analysis that not merely has the education system been skewed in class terms even more firmly since the Education Reform Act of 1988 through the expansion of parental choice, the reduction of the influence of professional, Local Education Authority (LEA) expertise and the seemingly admirable principle of expanded parental partnership, but that the National Curriculum has been constructed in a way that marginalises treatment of the more 'political' equality issues. The terms 'race', 'class' and 'sexuality' are almost impossible to find in subject documentation. Even the embrace of 'cultural diversity' is grudging and non-statutory- perhaps this shows that even this indirect and a-political approach to racial justice in the classroom has been more significant than its antiracist detractors understandably allege (Troyna and Williams, 1986).

Educating for Awareness of the Process of Exclusion

If this analysis is correct, there is a need to help teachers, who are after all overwhelmingly middle class in their origins as well as their professional status, become more aware of the class bias in almost all the work that they do. That is why the Didsbury Centre for Education for Equality has now created Study Packs at primary and secondary school levels to help foster and deepen student awareness of the wide range of elements that confirm and constantly recreate inequality and injustice in our society (Grinter, 1997). The Packs provide materials and commentaries that cover race, culture, class, gender, sexuality as well as physical disabilities. However, materials on class form a central element, and the commentaries stress that this characteristic of our '30/30/40' society, to use Will Hutton's phrase from an article that introduces that section of the Packs (Hutton, 1995), underpins all the other factors denying pupils their full life chances. Identifying with the life experiences and needs of groups of children less fortunate than ourselves is one of the most challenging tasks for all teachers, and regrettably one of which their background and life experience make many teachers almost totally unaware. It must be a priority task for anyone working for more equal outcomes from education, and tie in with mandatory elements of experience of working in an inner-city and/or multiracial school. A central part of teachers' understanding of inequality needs to be related to the processes by which this is created, and the part that schools, and therefore they themselves play in these processes. In the simplest terms a process operates by which members of selected social groups - women, lower skilled working people, black people, gays, lesbians, those with disabilities, and in Western societies the elderly- are devalued by stereotyping and then discriminated against. The discriminating process acquires some kind of 'justification' from the apparent inferiority of those in the groups concerned. A few in society remain untouched by the process, and it is no coincidence that these are the group at the head of our social system - white, heterosexual, male and professionally-educated. It is equally no surprise that this is the group that makes the rules, and has, therefore created the system and maintains the operation of the process that preserves it. Little wonder that the National Curriculum has so little reference to race, class, sexuality or stereotyping. What is surprising is how many intelligent and otherwise socially concerned people go along with this process, and in fact contribute to it.

This most certainly includes teachers: after all, if they teach fully to a National Curriculum that does not directly refer to this process, nor in positive terms to many of those who are on its receiving end and are in their classrooms, then they are hiding the process from their pupils. They are almost certainly confirming stereotypes of the varying worth of different categories of people, because these valuations are not just present in offensive terms and illustrations, but equally effective in the negative roles of members of these groups in the curriculum, or their total omission from it. If pupils never hear of the achievements of black people in African history or technological innovation, and only meet them as helpless objects of exploitation in the Atlantic Slave Trade, then the low valuation of black British people is obvious to everyone by implication and the operation of the discriminating process is powerfully confirmed. If teachers are not actively engaged in contesting this process, they are actively part of it, and whether they are unwitting agents or open discriminators matters little: the outcome is the same. Pupils are excluded from the expectations they deserve, and their aspirations and ambitions are correspondingly lowered. Awareness of this process of exclusion is, therefore, one of the two 'Key Concepts' in the commentaries in the Didsbury Study Packs.

Educating for Inclusion

The other 'Key Concept' in the Packs is Inclusion, which has recently become one of the key themes of New Labour. But in the context of this chapter and the work of the Didsbury Centre, it means the inclusion in the education process and the benefits that flow from it, of all groups - the full implementation of the most important word in the National Curriculum documentation for educators for equality, the 'entitlement' of all pupils to its benefits. That can only be done by subverting its structure because that structure was designed by people who had no full understanding of the processes that deny full entitlement, and who created a structure whose means denied the end they proclaimed. Anyone who doubts this only needs to consider whether there would be any difference if the National Curriculum was genuinely linked to the experiences of working class, black, gay and lesbian pupils, and to the real, if hidden, aspirations of many female pupils.

Because the National Curriculum is in many ways an ethnocentric document, the Didsbury Centre has made a priority of developing 'Guidelines' that assist teachers in identifying where opportunities to educate for equality do exist in National Curriculum subject documentation (Centre for Education for Equality, 1995). They show how gender issues can be fully incorporated in the National Curriculum, and how positive responses to the special needs of children with disabilities can be required throughout. These are easily identified. However, there are, as already noted, few direct and clear references to race and class, and a very varied treatment of cultural issues in different subject disciplines. But there are a surprisingly large number of references, albeit fleeting and not designed for the purpose, that can be used as opportunities to educate for equality in these crucial areas of education for equality. These are identified in the Guidelines, and were the subject of the author's paper to the first University of Hertfordshire Conference on Equality Issues in Education (Grinter, 1997). It is encouraging to see many recent publications that go beyond that initial analysis and suggest realistic ways of teaching that exploit the opportunities that do exist to subvert the curriculum structure to actively promote concern for a more equal society.

One effective way to show the implications of inclusion as a key educational principle is to define it as the guarantee of human rights to all pupils, paralleling the guarantee of human rights to all in the communities and social groups to which they belong. Human rights seem to most people in this country to be an issue concerning places like Somalia, Iraq, Indonesia and indeed any country except Bosnia outside the First World. The fact that homeless people and anyone suffering racism in this country are equally deprived of their human rights is less easily seen, as is the fact that bullied, racially harassed and indeed excluded pupils are losing their fundamental right as human beings to an education that will prepare them for a prosperous and happy life in the future. But to cast the issues of education for equality in these terms is to offer the basic justification for addressing all causes of inequality and deprivation of entitlement as a 'package'.

Almost every established social system survives on a basic strategy of divide and rule, and nothing causes those who benefit from it more quiet satisfaction than critics who mount separate campaigns for related purposes, and spend much of their energy condemning their potential colleagues who sometimes seem worse enemies than the system from which they all suffer. On the Left it was ever so. It was in this spirit that (Grinter, 1985) pleaded for an end to the divisive fratricidal warfare raging at that time between multiculturalists and antiracists, and for a focus on an 'antiracist multiculturalism'. This chapter is in some senses a continuation of that theme, but this time seeking to embrace a still more diverse set of campaigns, in which internecine warfare will quite certainly mean that some needs are excluded or downgraded. One of the main justifications for an inclusive and comprehensive approach is to ensure that that doesn't happen.

The range of concerns does create a still greater number of apparent reasons for divergence. But another of the virtues of an inclusive approach is that it does force campaigners to focus on their shared beliefs and concerns, and address the potential causes of conflict. This isn't easy, and calls for rather different skills than the campaigning against identified enemies. These diplomatic and consensus-building skills are not often the strengths of campaigners, but they are essential to unified action. These potential conflicts, the skills that are needed to deflect them and the pitfalls that await failure to address them will be the focus of the remainder of this chapter.

Avoiding Pitfalls: Identifying and Exploiting Links

It is important to explore what potential conflicts exist between issue groups, what links exist between the various issues, and assess whether these new gulfs in education for equality can be bridged. It will not be easy, any more than the efforts for more mutual understanding between multiculturalists and antiracists, and will only succeed if changes of perspective take place in the thinking of each group. But circumstances may well force change, as has certainly been the case in the earlier debate.

Some links have already been explored in the initial analysis of the central role of class. This demonstrated the link with the experience of racial prejudice, and some of the outcomes, including the exclusion of demoralised and angry pupils from the black British community. Further links here include the other side of the coin of the well-known variation in the level of achievement of ethnic minority pupils (Gillborn and Gipps, 1996). It is no coincidence that the 'over-achieving' groups, Hindus, Sikhs, Chinese and West Africans, are among the most professionally qualified community groups in the country.

The value of making this link is immediately apparent when we consider that the presence of the last of those communities in the list of high achievers must finally nail the lie that African pupils and communities suffer from some kind of cultural deficiency: instead it underlines the well-known fact that educational achievement in Western society depends to a large extent on having middle class, educated and reasonably affluent parents. This is confirmed by the fact that the other 'under-achieving' group in the analysis is Bangladeshi pupils; clearly a written cultural tradition does not guarantee academic success when a community is experiencing massive rates of unemployment and poverty. An exploration of links here will evidently do a great deal to re-establish some degree of decency in views of different cultural traditions.

Differences in the performance of the genders in the black British community have already been linked to the class context. Cultural factors may also make their contribution to the more conventional pattern of under-achievement of girls from some British Asian communities, particularly the Islamic community, where education is regarded more with anxiety as to its impact on the traditional culture than with confidence as a mean to personal and communal progress and prosperity. Relationships between dimensions of inequality can be complex and contradictory.

Another evident link is that between bullying and racism, where cultural differences are often the trigger points for persecution, as the tragic fate of Vijay Singh in Trafford highlighted (Halsall, 1996). The nature of the relationship between racism and other forms of bullying has underlined for us that bullying not only uses derogatory terminology to devalue potential victims, but sets up a process where stereotypes - in the case of Vijay Singh and many others, the inaccurate racial stereotype 'Paki' - are employed to secure the assent of onlookers who might otherwise intervene to protect and ensure justice.

An instructive set of links exists between culture and physical disabilities, where pupils with special educational needs from ethnic communities experience particular forms of illness which teachers need to be aware of such as sickle cell anaemia, thalassaemia and Tay-sach's syndrome that afflict the Afro-Caribbean, Cypriot and Jewish communities respectively. Additionally, their culture involves communication problems in linguistic terms, their experience of racism may well trigger or worsen behavioural difficulties, especially for boys. Here, once again the potential value of an approach that seeks to draw in all connected factors is clear: it enriches understanding and enhances the possibility of using strategies that are fully sensitive and have a chance of being fully effective.

Conclusion: Resolving Conflicts

Can this more comprehensive approach resolve the conflicts it highlights? Can it at least address issues in a way that those committed to separate campaigns can respect? The difficulties are self-evident, but probably only fully understandable to those who have experienced stereotyping and discrimination personally. But it must help in tackling difficulties to realise how complex the system of stereotyping and devaluation is, and how it sets people in similar situations against each other.

For example, black men and black women both suffer racism, but black men are no less sexist than white men - and black feminists are presumably no more forgiving of sexism than white feminists, wherever it comes from. When different cultures in a mixed society embody different views of the roles and rights of women, misunderstanding and intolerance are only too likely; it is easy for white feminists to be seen as racist in their disapproval of other cultural norms (Arora, 1988), and black men's antiracism to be seen as tainted by sexism. In a more specifically racial context, the integrity and depth and range of the understanding of white, male, liberal professionals in the field of work for equality must always be suspect to those who feel the impact of racial prejudice and discrimination more directly.

In wider terms it is difficult for anyone to move out of a context which is part of one's whole identity, and take on board the hurt and anger and needs of other groups of people. It must be even more difficult when some actions of members of those groups contribute to one's own experience of discrimination. Equally, it must be very difficult for members of all groups experiencing discrimination to work with people who are linked to, and benefit from, the system that creates misfortune for others. The benefit of a coherent, inclusive and wide-ranging approach could be that it demands that conflicts are addressed, and requires everyone to consider with greater understanding the situations of those they cannot fully trust or relate to. But unusual qualities and an unusual range of sympathies are required for this to happen.

This is not to claim that anyone engaged in this wider-ranging approach to work against inequality is wiser, better or shrewder than others. No system and no perspective creates virtue. A commitment to human rights is no guarantee of universal respect or effective strategy, especially when an activist is perfectly secure in his, or, less often, her personal rights. The wider the range of concerns, the more danger there is of a vague well-meaningness: the accusation has been made often enough and there is no smoke without fire.

Any more wide-ranging strategy certainly cannot replace separate campaigns, and must not weaken their impact. But a wide range of concerns can help to broaden everyone's understanding and sensitivities. For teachers it can provide a basis to respond even more effectively to the complex and varied needs of children. It underlines that children cannot be treated alike because many inhabit and respond to worlds whose complexity their teachers can only begin to grasp. The case for a wide-ranging approach that this chapter attempts to make may well meet insuperable obstacles in the 'real world', and many conflicts may not be capable of resolution. But the strategy can help to create a sensitivity to the complexity of experiences of children as members of their communities, may enable teachers to identify more closely with the reality of their pupils' needs, and make even more significant contributions to helping them meet them effectively.

Bibliography

Arora, R. (1998), *Race and Gender in Education* (unpublished paper), Race Relations Research Unit, Bradford and Ilkley College, UK.

Centre for Education for Equality (1995), *Education for Equality Study Packs*, Didsbury School of Education, Manchester Metropolitan University, UK.

Centre for Education for Equality (1995), *Guidelines for Education for Equality Areas of the National Curriculum*, Didsbury School of Education, Manchester Metropolitan University, UK.

Cole, M. (1989), *Education for Equality: Some Guidelines for Good Practice*, Routledge, London.

Cole, M. Hill, D. and Shan, S. (1997), *Promoting Equality in Primary Schools*, Cassell, London.

Cole. M, Hill, D. and Shan, S. (1997), *Promoting Equality in Secondary Schools*, Cassell, London.

Gaine, C. (1995), *Still No Problem Here*, Trentham, Stoke-on-Trent, UK.

George, R. (1993), A Handbook on Equal Opportunities in Schools: Principles, Policy and Practice, Longman, London.

Gillborn, D. and Gipps, C. (1996), *Recent Research into the Achievement of Ethnic Minority Groups*, OFSTED, HMSO, London

Grinter, R. (1997), 'Using the National Curriculum to Educate for Equality', pp. 51-7 in Shah, S. (ed), *National Initiatives and Equality Issues*, Centre for Equality Issues in Education, University of Hertfordshire, UK.

Halsall, M. (1986), 'Hanged Boy Told of Bullying in Poems', in *The Guardian*, October 13.

Hattersley, R. (1996), 'Balance of Power', in *The Guardian*, July 25.

Hutton, W. (1995), 'The 30/30/40 Society', in *The Guardian*, October 30.

Illich, Ivan (1971), *Deschooling*, Penguin, London.

Klein, G. (1993), *Education Towards Race Equality*, Cassell, London.

Potts, P. and Arm, F. (1995), *Equality and Diversity in Education: Learning, Teaching and Managing in Schools*, Routledge, London.

Reiser, R. and Mason, M. (1990), *Disability Education in the Classroom: A Human Rights Issue*, Inner London Education Authority, London.

Roberts, H. (1994), *Teaching from an Equality Perspective*, Sage, London.

Riley, K. (1994), *Quality and Equality: Promoting Opportunities in School*, Cassell, London.

Singh, G. (1993), *Equality and Education*, Albrighton, London.

Smith, D. (1997), *Racial Disadvantage in Britain*, Policy Studies Institute, London.

Troyna, B. and Williams, J. (1986), *Racism, Education and the State*, Croom Helm, London.

Wigley, J. (1992), *Education and Gender Equality*, Falmer, London.

3 Gender and Race: Maintaining and Crossing Boundaries

SNEH SHAH

Abstract

The 1970s were critical from the point of equality issues in the United Kingdom. Two important pieces of legislation were passed and two organisations were set up to support the work to be undertaken in the fields of gender and race. However, the two organisations and the legislation, although broadly under the umbrella of equality, had different agendas and pressure groups within the country.

Generally speaking, in the 1970s and 1980s the two bodies and majority of educationists kept issues of gender and race separate. In the 1990s, however, there have been important examples of collaboration between the two organisations, and clear evidence that each one is beginning to make links with what was traditionally seen as the work of the other. There has also been a clear attempt to have greater influence on policy by co-operating to make links with bodies responsible for the formulation and implementation of education policy. Various factors have led to collaboration. The work of each organisation has also included integration. However, integration between gender and race issues is still limited.

The chapter also examines the value of organisations such as Commission for Racial Equality (CRE) and Equal Opportunities Commission (EOC), which focus on one specific strand of equality within the context of integration, and discusses some possible future developments, including the place of specific strands under the umbrella of human rights.

Distinct Origins and Agendas

The 1970s were a critical period for race and gender, as they winessed the setting up of the legislative framework and other supportive organisations which are, with some amendments, still in force. However, although both had a focus on disadvantage, the agendas of the Commission for Racial Equality (CRE) and the Equal Opportunities Commission (EOC) reflect distinct pressure groups and philosophies that initially lacked any integration between race and gender.

Gender as Equal Opportunities

The field of equality is riddled with terms which are often assumed to be interchangeable, yet which sometimes create rather than clear confusion. Equal opportunities is a good example of such a term. It has often been used to refer to gender only, and even within the context of gender, to issues concerning girls and women only. For instance, the early documents for the individual subjects in the National Curriculum used equal opportunities as meaning achievements of boys and girls. The usage of the term reflects the reasons why concern was raised and sex discrimination legislation was passed: to bring the level of pay and performance of women to the same level as that of men.

Earlier concerns and legislation were strengthened by the passing of the Sex Discrimination Act in 1975 which also set up the Equal Opportunities Commission. It makes sex discrimination unlawful in the provision of employment, education, and goods, facilities and services. Two forms of discrimination are described in the Act, direct and indirect, both of which are unlawful. The provisions of the Act apply equally to discrimination against either sex, and not just girls and women.

There was, however, no reference to race in the early dialogues and developments in the field of gender equality. The movements for equality for women came from white groups, who saw no connection between their work and that of pressure groups working on racial issues.

Race Relations

The need for legislation and a regulatory framework for race relations had been talked about since the 1940s, broadly parallel to the granting of independence to the New Commonwealth countries, and the arrival in Britain of significant numbers of non-European immigrants. The pressure for action came from two sources. One was the recurrence of so-called riots which frightened politicians and urged them to take action. The other main source of pressure was some of the non-European minority ethnic groups, in particular Afro-Caribbean communities. They often took inspiration from developments in the United States of America. The setting up of bodies such as National Committee for Commonwealth Immigrants, Commonwealth Immigrants' Advisory Council, Race Relations Board and Race Relations Commission, and two earlier race relations acts were replaced by the 1976 Race Relations Act, which set up the Commission for Racial Equality. The terms of reference of the 1976 Race Relations Act were much wider; it covered direct discrimination and indirect discrimination, and underlined victimisation. Complaints by individuals were facilitated, and codes of practice were to be introduced.

Issues of race were acknowledged and put on the agenda for action be some non-European minority ethnic groups and individuals from others. Their approach was often related to the structures and power base in society which were racist. The remit of the CRE is, therefore, much broader than that of the EOC. The CRE publicises its work (CRE, nd) as:

> working for a just society which gives everyone an equal chance to learn, work and live free from discrimination and prejudice, and from the fear of racial harassment and violence.

In response to the pressures from communities, but in particular so-called riots and disturbances in the second half of the twentieth century, British governments tried to take action. But their agendas were generally different from those of the minority communities. The approach to racism was in many ways designed to control the effect of the presence of minorities in British society. The speech by Roy Jenkins in 1966 to the Committee for Commonwealth Immigrants is a clear indication of how governments, regardless of their political party beliefs, saw race (Law, 1996, p.12):

> I do not think we need in this country a melting pot which will turn everybody out in a common mould, as one of a series of carbon copies of someone's misplaced version of a stereotyped Englishmen ... I define integration, therefore, not as a flattening process of assimilation but as equal opportunity, coupled with cultural diversity, in an atmosphere of mutual tolerance.

The legislation was designed to give a particular nature to the society in which immigrants were to be 'integrated'. Law (1996) refers to the 'peripheralisation of policy and management with respect to domestic racism', which is a persistent feature in Britain. In addition, there was no reference in the debates on legislation to integration with gender or other issues of equality.

Nature of Integration between CRE and EOC

There were attempts, especially in the 1990s, to acknowledge the commonality between gender and race issues, and the value of the organisations co-operating.

Collaboration

Examples of collaboration are very practical. The best examples of collaboration are publications, firstly for managers in Further Education (Commission for Racial Equality et al, 1995), and secondly, for managers in Higher Education (Commission for Racial Equality et al, 1997). Collaboration has extended to other organisations, for instance, with the Further Education Funding Council for the first publication, and the Committee for Vice-Chancellors and Principals for the second one. These are designed to encourage and support institutions to have effective equal opportunity policies. At the same time, developments from other organisations are given support. For instance collaboration with the Commission on University Career Opportunity (CUCO) has been important for institutional approaches to harassment.

Content Integration

There has been an increasing number of examples of integration within the work of the individual organisations. However, issues of race have normally focused on ethnicity, and issues of gender on minority ethnic women, with some exceptions such as the education of Afro-Caribbean boys and young men.

Within the Equal Opportunities Commission, the focus has generally been minority ethnic women and the labour market (e.g. Bhavnani, 1994; Owen, 1994). Such work is also raising new items for the quality agenda.

Bhavnani (1994, p.12) sees greater complexity than has been normally stated for minority ethnic women:

> Black women's experiences cannot always assumed to be different from white women, black men or white men in all contexts. The cross-cutting of such factors as race, gender, class and agecreate a multiplicity of discrimination. In some contexts there may be similarities as well as differences between white women and black and white men.

Bhavnani (1994) also points out the dynamic nature of the different cultural and structural factors, rendering terms such as West Indian and Asian as misguiding and unhelpful. The interlinking of various factors - gender, race, culture, class, age - require new terminology.

One major project underlining integration has been undertaken by the Commission for Racial Equality, called Visible Women: Challenging Race and Sex Discrimination. As the first national campaign about ethnic minority women in Britain, it aims to publicise the main issues of concern to minority ethnic women, increase general awareness of the barriers that prevent equal access, especially in the labour market, and to dispel existing stereotypes mainly by detailing successes of a range of women within different contexts.

Integration in relation to gender and race is thus limited, but the work undertaken by the CRE and EOC so far has only started unwinding the complexity of the issues. They are not static and a true appreciation of the position of different groups of people in society requires a constant revision of the frameworks and terminology.

Value of Combining CRE and EOC

There have been discussions about the merger of the two organisations. There appear to be some advantages, but significant disadvantages, and lack of clear agreement has meant the two will probably continue their separate existence in the foreseeable future.

Advantages

The advantages stem from the fact that there are significant fundamental barriers in education institutions to effective implementation of meaningful equal opportunity policies. The changes CRE and EOC would like to see in relation to education institutions are similar. While there is generally greater resistance to greater racial equality, individuals in power have been socialised into creating and supporting structures in their institutions that generally endorse male and white superiority. Thus when they are supported by funding/quality control bodies, EOC and CRE are more likely to have better response from education managers.

The lack of normal dialogue about the interlinking of gender and race issues points to a reversal of the situation if the two organisations were merged. For instance, what is generally perceived to be a key feature of a relationship between gender and race is described quite aptly by Frankenburg (1993) as 'race shapes white women's lives'. Research and projects into minority ethnic women are only a very small aspect of a comprehensive approach to equality. Bringing the organisations together can lead to debates not just about the structures of the organisations but their philosophies. This would mean a more comprehensive analysis of how gender and race impact upon individuals, communities, and British society as a whole.

Problems with Integration

However, collaboration does not necessarily mean integration of the two organisations. Although both the organisations have been in existence for some years, what they have been able to achieve has been limited, partly due to the level of resources that has been made available to them. Joining the two organisations may not necessarily mean a continuation of the level of resources allocated to the two organisations separately, and the probability is that it may be lowered. Similarities between their tasks should not imply, but politicians may take the line that, a reduction in resource allocation is justified.

The recent joint publications have underlined the need for the organisations to work together. However, in both the areas of race and gender much work needs to be done separately. Yu (1998/1999) is critical of developments in Northern Ireland as the setting up of the new Equalities Commission has been done without enough case-law being built up especially by the Commission for Racial Equality (Northern Ireland). Thus a new organisation will need to have scope for specific issues being investigated and acted upon separately, as well as an emphasis on holistic projects.

Gender, Race and Human Rights

An approach being adopted elsewhere is related to human rights. The passing of the Human Rights Act in 1998 brings United Kingdom in line with the European Union on human rights. An overarching approach can enable not only greater links between race and gender, but a proper focus for other aspects of equality such as class and age. The approach adopted by Northern Ireland appears to both allow for continued separate exploration of gender and race issues and create a framework for adequate interlinking. However, it will become clear in the future if the advantages of having a single Commission to cover different strands of equal opportunities will materialise, in view of the fact that no added resources have been made available to the Commission.

Cooper (1998) finds the Human Rights Act disappointing as it does not guarantee a free-standing right to equality. There is a recognition of the rights to freedom from discrimination, but this only applies to rights recognised by the Human Rights Convention. Discrimination, unless it applies to a Convention right, would not be considered a human rights issue. However, extreme discriminatory treatment on the basis of race is held to amount to inhuman and degrading treatment. Thus the Human Rights Act does not add to the widening of what is encompassed by the term equality. It does, however, enable more individuals to take legal action if they feel they are being disadvantaged. Higher education institutions in the United Kingdom are already organising adequate insurance cover for an anticipated increase in student complaints once the Act comes into force in the year 2000.

Conclusion

Collaboration between EOC and CRE has been important in putting equality on the agenda for education institutions. However, major changes need to take place. For instance, the need for a revision of the Race

Relations Act has been discussed at length, but the various British governments have refused to take any action. The work, power and resources of both CRE and EOC need to be strengthened. However, if the two organisations were merged, that will need to be done on the basis of a wider remit for each one of them but under one umbrella to help both the debates and policies to move forward. Equally integration would have to have a forum for definitions and ongoing discussions of equality issues.

The type of content integration that has taken place indicates an urgent need for a more open, dynamic debate at the highest levels. It needs to take into account the ever-changing nature of equality issues which embrace other strands such as disability, class and age. Law (1996) refers to the changing nature of identities in relation to race, gender and class, but that needs to be expanded to include contexts and consequences.

Especially with its project on Roots to the Future, CRE has placed a key part in beginning to turn the focus away from disadvantage to enrichment. This is echoed by Hoskyns (1996, p. 167):

> ... being black, migrant and a woman in the EU means not an accumulation of discriminations but a particular experience of society, disadvantageous in some ways but rich in others, and with its own internal contradictions and diversities.

Both the organisations need to be alert that the Human Rights Act does not take the pressure away from structural changes in society. While the rule of law provides a potentially strong argument for challenging racism and sexism, Law (1996, p. 8) reminds us:

> Yet conceptions of individual liberty can also provide the basis for challenging attempts to tackle the structural barriers of social inequality where there is a concern for group inequality.

In many ways, whether there are two separate organisations or not, is thus immaterial. What is more crucial is that EOC and CRE become more central to policy decisions by governments, at the same time as initiating and supporting a critical ongoing dialogue so that the separate strands of gender and race become much more powerful and better interconnected.

Bibliography

Barot, R., Bradley, H. and Fenton, S. (eds) (1999), *Ethnicity, Gender and Social Change*, Macmillan, London.

Bhavnani, R. (1994), *Black Women in the Labour Market: A Research Review*, Equal Opportunities Commission, Manchester, UK.

Brown, C. (1984), *Black and White Britain: The Third PSI Survey*, Policy Studies Institute, London.

Brown, M. (1999), 'Service Please', in *Connections*, Spring, pp. 10-12.

Collins, H.(1992), *The Equal Opportunities Handbook: A Guide to Law and Best Practice in Europe*, Blackwell, London.

Commission for Racial Equality, Equal Opportunities Commission and Committee of Vice-Chancellors and Principals (1997), *Higher Education and Equality: A Guide*, CRE, EOC and CVCP, London.

Commission for Racial Equality and Equal Opportunities Commission (1995), Further *Education and Equality: A Managers Manual*, CRE and EOC, London.

Commission for Racial Equality (no date), *No Limits - Visible Women, Challenging Race and Sex Discrimination*, publication of the Visible Women Campaign, CRE, London.

Cooper, J. (1998), 'Defining Human Rights', in *The Runnymede Bulletin*, no. 316, Nov./Dec., pp. 6-7.

Commission for Racial Equality (no date), *What is the Commission for Racial Equality?*, CRE, London.

Editorial (1999), 'EOC Rules OK? Oh No!', in *New Impact Journal*, vol. 5, pp. 6-8.

Equal Opportunities Commission (1988), *Black and Ethnic Minority Women in Britain: a Review of Demographic and Employment Patterns*, Internal Research Unit Paper, EOC, Manchester, UK.

Frankenberg, R. (1993), *The Social Construction of Whiteness: White Women, Race Matters*, Routledge, London.

Hoskyns, C. (1996), *Integrating Gender: Women, Law and Politics in the European Union*, Verso.

Law, I. (1996), *Racism, Ethnicity and Social Policy*, Prentice-Hall/Harvester Wheatsheaf, Hemel Hempstead, Hertfordshire, UK.

Owen, D. (1994), *Ethnic Minority Women and the Labour Market: Analysis of the 1991 Census*, EOC, Manchester, UK.

Spence, S. and Bynoe, I. (1996/1997), 'Human Rights Protection: Lessons from History', in *The Runnymede Bulletin*, Dec/Jan 1996/7, no. 299, pp. 2-4.

Yu, P. (1998/1999), 'Equal Rights for Racial Equality', in *Connections*, Winter, Commission for Racial Equality, p. 10.

4 Asian Women Undergraduates and their Attitudes to British Schooling: A Complex Issue

HARKIRTAN SINGH-RAUD

Abstract

Institutions have to bear in mind that education is for all. Hence they need to be aware of and understand the characteristics of various cultural and religious backgrounds of their students of Asian origin. It is essential to understand the complex patterns of cultural development and religious practices, even within the so-called 'Asian' group. This chapter explores the relationship between religious backgrounds and the attitudes of Asian women undergraduates towards education. It is important for ethnocentric institutions to learn that South-east Asian girls are not a homogeneous assemblage. They are discernible, for instance, by religion, sect, linguistic association, caste and country of origin.

The research conducted by Harkirtan Singh-Raud found that although there were commonalties between the three religious groups studied (i.e. Hindus, Muslims and Sikhs), there were differences that were evident in some of the responses of the undergraduates that may show the influence of religion. The conclusion is that if schools in Britain fail to understand the dissimilar effects of religion on ethnic minority students, then South-east Asian students will experience a degree of 'creedism' and lack of support due to the non-religious aligned suppositions.

What Singh-Raud's study raises are other critical issues which have to be understood by educational institutions. The use of terms such as Asian and South-east Asian has become common, but the accuracy of those terms has to be judged in the specific contexts of study and may not be easily transferable. It also leaves educationalists with the real challenge of understanding the effect of the specific group membership on the individual student, yet accepting that that person is still an individual. Breaking down stereotyping in a whole group could create further stereotypes.

Introduction

The primary aim of this chapter is to explore the attitudes towards school education of Asian women, especially those in higher education who form a significant role model in the wider context of the development of British plural society.

Although the terms Asian or South-east Asian are used throughout, they need some explanation. Asian is a term used, in the United Kingdom, to represent a person whose origins are from either India, Pakistan, Bangladesh, Sri Lanka or is the descendant of those who originally migrated to East African countries from the Indian sub-continent. The term Asian is predominately used in the United States of America to refer to people who originate from China, Korea, Taiwan, Japan, Thailand and other countries which we, in the United Kingdom, are regarded as the Far East (Singh-Raud, 1997a). As Ghuman (1975) suggests it is a term that is not very informative because it covers cultural differences as great as those between widely separated European countries. It is so broad that in fact culturally a Madrasi Indian girl is considerably different from a Bengali Indian girl. However, a Punjabi Muslim girl from Pakistan would culturally have a great deal in common with a Punjabi Sikh girl from India, for example, in the language spoken, style of cooking, style of music, style of clothing worn etc. Hence to say that a person is an Asian is in fact quite ambiguous. However, for the purposes of this study the definition of an Asian as given by Madood and Shiner (1994) is used, that an Asian person is one who 'shares in the heritages of the civilisations of old Hindustan prior to British conquest' and is one of those who 'believe that the Taj Mahal is an object of their history'.

Research Project

Subjects were identified using 'stratified sampling' (Cohen and Manion,1994). Various university departments were contacted and informed of the research, and requested to allow sometime at the start of their lectures, to explain the research to their students. The Asian women students were then asked to complete the questionnaire in their own time and leave it at the reception. The completed questionnaires were collected at the end of the day. Initially departments that had high levels of Asian women students were approached. These included departments of law, medicine, pharmacy, science, and education. There was a clear bias against the 'Arts' but a rudimentary survey discovered that the number of students of South-east Asian origin found on the 'Arts' courses was very small (Woodrow, 1996) and therefore would prove to be an inefficient use of resources.

The research was being conducted in the North-West of England but it was found that the initial sample of one hundred and three predominantly Muslims was not proportionally representative of the population found in this part of England. Another problem was that the initial sample contained a very small proportion of Sikh and Hindu women. To counter-act this problem, the way sampling was conducted had to be changed to a form of 'quota sampling' (Cohen and Manion, 1994). Hence universities in areas that contained high numbers of Sikhs and Hindus were approached. These were in the Midlands and the South of England. To get a 'fairer' sample the students unions were approached and the questionnaire was personally administered to each respondent, and the research explained. This yielded a sample that contained fifty-one Sikh respondents, fifty-two Hindu respondents (including Jains), and ninety-nine Muslim respondents, giving a total population of two hundred and two respondents.

The data was statistically analysed, using SPSS, in terms of its significance, and the findings are presented as descriptive and interpretative. The test used for significance was a non-parametric test known as the 'Kolmogorov-Smirnov Z, 2-independent samples' Test (Seigal, 1956). This was accomplished by firstly entering all the data and then using for tests of significance the three variables namely 'Hindu', 'Muslim' and 'Sikh'. These were used to compare the differences between a particular group, e.g. 'Hindu', and the two others combined. Hence the *Grouping Variable* was one of the named 'extra' variable e.g. 'Hindu' and hence its define groups were 1 for Hindu and 2 for Muslim and Sikh, therefore, comparing Hindus with the others. The *Test Variable* was the question being tested. A 'P' Value of 0.05 was used to indicate that the data was significant (Singh-Raud, 1997a). As with most individual research the sample size could not be large enough to *guarantee* the results being representative of the population at large.

Nevertheless, the issues that have arisen clearly have an existence within the community and in one sense the validity is ensured by the expression of those concerns. The sample size was chosen to be large enough to remove isolated idiosyncrasies and to provide for the checking of witness statements against other contributors. Since the focus was largely questionnaire, care was taken to have a reasonable number and a reasonable balance of respondents. The extent to which this reasonableness is valid will always be open to question but the commonality of views which emerged gives the researcher confidence that these views have general currency.

In seeking Hindu, Muslim and Sikh respondents it was found that they were grouped in communities rather than spread through the higher education system. No attempt has been made to uncover regional and/or institutional biases that may have occurred as a consequence though clearly a larger study would need to address such a variable and this study provides data from which valid questions could be posed.

Results

Strength of Religious Belief

It was found that in general 73 per cent of the total sample regarded themselves as religiously moderate. However, there was a (non-significant) tendency for the Sikh respondents to be less religious than their counter parts ($p=0.081$). Again, 73 per cent of the university respondents said that their families were also moderates. Yet 25 per cent of the Hindu women and 20 per cent of the Muslim women held that their family were strongly religious. This is in contrast with the school finding where 9 per cent of the Hindu girls felt that their family was strongly religious. It should be noted that no evaluation was made of the strength of religiosity, these were self-declared and self-assessed measures. Clearly, however, fundamentalists would wish to declare their commitment. Significant differences were found between the three religious groups as to who was the most religious member of the family.

For the majority of the Muslim respondents, the fathers (41 per cent: $p=0.00$) were the most religious members of the family. They were more religious than Hindu (12 per cent) and Sikh (12 per cent) fathers. Whereas for the Hindus (65 per cent) and Sikhs (67 per cent) it was the mother who was the most religious member of the family. This is probably because the Muslim fathers see themselves as the guardians of the faith. Whereas in the Hindu and Sikh communities the women take an active role in prayers and temple 'pooja' (worship). This pattern was repeated in the main school study findings.

It appeared that Muslim women (28 per cent:$p=0.01$) became more religious after religious after arriving at university, whereas the Hindu (94 per cent) and Sikh (92 per cent) women were of the opinion that they were unchanged in their level of belief or had become less religious since arriving at university. This may be because Muslim women feel threatened about their religion in the Western world. Haw (1994) found that controversial issues such as the Honeyford affair, the Dewsbury and Cleveland cases, Salman Rushdie's book, the Gulf War, and the 1988 Education Reform Act have all served to sharpen the community's sense of awareness of its own identity and its belief in separating Muslim culture and Islam from the permissive contemporary British society. Hence they turn to their religion for security. Naipaul (1982) has noted that since the Iranian revolution of 1980 and the resurgence of Islam as a proselytising religion, Muslims in many countries have felt more confident in asserting their community and religious values. However, it could also be that at university the British Muslims meet Muslims from other parts of the world and begin to align themselves more with their religion. Jacobson (1997) found that young British Pakistanis regarded religion as a more significant source of social identity than ethnicity because, she suggested, religion plays a more significant role in their lives. It could also be a consequence of Muslim women staying near their home community and being drawn, as adults, in direct personal commitment rather than the affiliation with religion which children draw upon.

Education in Schools

However, of the Muslim respondents, a significant minority (26 per cent) wanted single sex schooling, whereas this was only the case with 10 per cent of Hindu and Sikh women. Basit (1995) found that Muslim parents she studied preferred to have their daughters attend single-sex schools as there was an uninhibited environment in these schools. Ghuman (1993) reported that Muslim leaders held the view that single sex schools at the secondary stage were important for the healthy growth of their young people. However, he found that Hindus and Sikhs were less keen. They did not see them as a problem.

A highly significant minority (44 per cent:p=0.00) of Muslim women favoured separate religious schools as opposed to 10 per cent of Hindu women and 12 per cent of Sikh women respondents. Skinner (1990) has suggested that the Muslim community are eager to establish Muslim voluntary schools to avoid opting out into separate private schools and being able to take full advantage of the aided schools provisions within the maintained system. Parker-Jenkins (1991) also found that the Muslim community called for separate publicly funded schooling for Muslim children. This may be due to the reasons suggested by Haw (1994).

A majority of the Asian university women sample (86 per cent) wanted school children to wear school uniform. There was no significant difference between the three religious groups. One of the interviewees in the pilot study suggested that it minimized difference in dress and, therefore, brought more amity. A significant majority of the Muslim sample of university respondents (78 per cent) wanted school uniform to be modified for religious reasons whereas this was the case with only 28 per cent of the Hindu respondents and 50 per cent of the Sikh respondents. Verma et al. (1994) found that teachers believed in the importance of respecting religious belief and hence schools were responding sympathetically to the demands made by Muslim parents with regard to dress, and the earlier problems were somewhat dissipated.

Table 4.1   Significance of mother tongue (MT) teaching

Religion	Respondent taught MT at school		Respondent used MT at university		Respondent believed MT should be taught at school	
	Yes %	No %	Yes %	No %	Yes %	No %
Hindu	20	80	42	58	48	52
Muslim	19	81	61	39	49	51
Sikh	18	81	66	34	74	26

From table 4.1 it can be seen that 81 per cent of the sample had not been taught their mother-tongue in school. It should be noted that there was a tendency for the Hindu respondents (58 per cent) to not want their mother-tongue taught in schools, compared to 34 per cent of the Sikh respondents and 39 per cent of the Muslim respondents. This may be due to the fact that it is more common for Hindus to speak English at home than the other two groups. The Hindu elders are usually fluent in English and hence there is n real communication barrier when conversing in English. This would clearly diminish the significance of the mother tongue. Drury (1991) found that Sikh girls favoured the teaching of the mother tongue in schools as this would help communication with the elders and would make them proud of their heritage.

Dhasmana (1994) reported that the Asian parents in his sample (almost entirely Muslim) wanted Urdu and Arabic taught in schools. There was a significant difference (p=0.02) between the three religious groups and the use of their mother-tongue at university. It was found that 74 per cent of the Sikh students used Punjabi, their mother tongue, at university whereas this was the case with 48 per cent and 49 per cent of Hindu and Muslim students respectively. A significant majority of the Muslim women students (85 per cent) were not satisfied with the level of religious education given in schools. This was the case with 59 per cent of the Sikh and 64 per cent of the Hindu respondents. In general, a majority of all the religious groups were dissatisfied with the level of religious instructions but clearly the most dissatisfied group were the Muslims.

This is probably related to the earlier finding that Muslim students become more religious after arriving at university whereas a majority of the Sikhs remain unchanged. Ghuman (1994) found that the Hindu and Sikh communities were far more 'lax/liberal' on the issue of religious instruction compared to the Muslim community.

There was a significant difference between the religious groups as to their attitude towards having sex education taught in school. A significant majority of the Sikhs respondents (86 per cent) wanted sex education taught with the remainder wanting it optional except for one respondent who did not want it taught. A significant minority of Muslim respondents (35 per cent) wanted sex education optional, three respondents did not want it to be taught and 61 per cent wanted it taught in school. Three quarters of the Hindu respondents wanted sex education taught in school and the remainder wanted it as optional. In recent research (Singh-Raud, 1997b) it was found that Sikh and Hindu girls wanted sex education taught but the Muslim girls wanted to have an option not to take it. A Muslim Teachers' Conference held in 1979 passed a resolution against sex education in schools on the grounds that sex education and sex aids are for people who are disillusioned with their own promiscuity (McDermott and Ahsan, 1986). In general the Asian university students wanted sex education to be taught whether it was compulsory or optional. With regard to Asian topics being part of the school curriculum, 55 per cent of the Muslim women, 53 per cent of the Sikh women and 35 per cent of the Hindu women wanted such a requirement (Table 4.2).

It was noted that a majority of the Hindu respondents, 55 per cent, 42 per cent of the Sikh respondents and 41 per cent of the Muslim respondents wanted Asian topics as optional, and the remainder did not want to see them on the school curriculum. However, the difference between the three religious groups was not significant. It can be seen that in general Asian university students (95 per cent) wanted to see Asian topics as part of the school curriculum; be they compulsory or optional. A majority of Asian girls in a recent study (Singh-Raud, 1997a) also wanted Asian topics taught in school.

Table 4.2 Asian topics in schools

Religion	Yes %	No %	Optional %
Hindu	35	10	55
Muslim	53	6	41
Sikh	55	3	42

There was a significant difference between the religious groups in their attitude towards having Asian dishes as part of the school lunch menu. A significant majority of the Muslim respondents (69 per cent: $p=0.00$) wanted Asian dishes on the school menu as compared to 49 per cent Sikh respondents and 29 per cent Hindu respondents. This is probably because, as Verma et al. (1994) found, Muslim students in school become fish eating vegetarians as a response to religious restrictions of only being allowed to eat 'Halal' meat (killed according to Islamic law). However, a significant majority of Hindu respondents (54 per cent: $p=0.00$) wanted Asian dishes as optional, compared to 47 per cent of the Sikhs and 29 per cent of the Muslim students. It can be seen that in general 94 per cent of the total sample wanted schools to provide Asian dishes as part of the menu or as an option. The university students did not feel they should be ashamed of Asian meals, especially since many of the indigenous population visit Indian restaurants.

It was found that 86 per cent of the whole sample wanted to see Asian teachers in school for various reasons. The majority stated equality, others felt that they provided role models or that they understood the Asian students better. The Swann Commitee (Department of Education and Science, 1985) had stressed the 'pastoral', 'role model' and 'cultural resources' values of the presence of black teachers in multiracial and all white schools. Verma et al. (1994) found that schools in the south of England tended to have more Asian staff (between one-sixth to one-fifth) whereas in the north the number of ethnic minority teachers was substantially smaller. With regard to having more Asian lecturers the findings were almost identical to that for the Asian school teachers.

Higher Education

With regard to encouragement to pursue higher education there was a significant difference between the Muslim sample of respondents and the Sikh and Hindu respondents. It was found that 50 per cent of the Muslim women had been encouraged by a matriarchal member of the family (mother, sister or aunt). Of the Muslim women, 29 per cent were encouraged by their fathers, and 13 per cent felt that no one encouraged them. Siann and Khalid (1984) discovered that their sample of Glasgow mothers were concerned that their daughters should receive as much education as possible with a view to supporting themselves in employment if the need arose. With the Hindu respondents, however, a significant 63 per cent were encouraged by their fathers, 15 per cent by their mother and 9 per cent by others. The remainder felt that they were not encouraged by any one. Like the Hindu women, the majority of Sikh respondents (47 per cent) felt that they were encouraged by their fathers, 27 per cent by their mothers and 8 per cent by others. The remainder were not encouraged by any one.

Tomlinson (1983) found that a majority of the black women in higher education she studied were encouraged by their fathers and the ones that were encouraged by their mothers came from single parent families. With regards to being discouraged from pursuing higher education the majority of the sample, 92 per cent Hindus, 78 per cent Sikhs and had been encouraged by a matriarchal member of the family (mother, sister or aunt). Of the Muslim women, 29 per cent were encouraged by their fathers and 13 per cent felt that no one encouraged them. With the Hindu respondents, however, a significant 63 per cent were encouraged by their fathers, 15 per cent by their mother and 9 per cent by others. The remainder felt that they were not encouraged by any one. Like the Hindu women, the majority of Sikh respondents (47 per cent) felt that they were encouraged by their fathers, 73 per cent Muslim respondents, were of the opinion that they had not been discouraged by anybody. However it was noticeable that 13 per cent of the Muslim sample had been discouraged by either the father or an uncle, whereas this was the case with only 4 per cent of the Sikh women and 2 per cent of the Hindu women. It was discovered that 79 per cent of the respondents had members of the family who had either been to university or were at present at university.

On the question of location of their university education there was a significant difference between the three religious groups. A significant majority of the Hindu women (73 per cent) moved away from home, to another city, for their university studies, while 6 per cent moved out of their home although they stayed in the home city. The remainder stayed at home while studying. In contrast, a significant majority of Muslim women (62 per cent) decided to reside at home while pursuing their university qualifications. A signifant number, 32 per cent of the Muslim respondents moved away from home and the remainder moved out of their home although they stayed in the home city. With respect to the Sikh respondents, there was almost a balanced split in that 43 per cent moved away to another city, 53 per cent stayed at home and 4 per cent moved out of their home but they stayed in the home city.

Although some students tended to stay at home for their studies, possibly due to financial reasons, there was a clear difference between the religious groups in that the Muslim women tended to stay at home for university studies whereas the Hindu and, to some extent, the Sikh women preferred to move away their city. Taylor (1993) found in his research that University Central Council on Admissions (UCCA) suggested that application to local institutions was more popular among ethnic minority groups and therefore restricted their choice and chances of acceptance. However, UCCA did not divulge the religious background of these students. Singh-Raud (1997) found from the pilot interviews that the Muslim women were allowed to pursue higher education on the condition that they went to their local university as one of the Muslim interviewees stated, 'My dad would not let me go out of Manchester and so I had to get in to Manchester Met. (Metropolitan University) or I couldn't go'.

Singh (1990, p. 346) suggested that:

> Some parents of South Asian girls may not encourage their daughters to study away from home in institutions which have no students of similar background or with an overall social/cultural environment which is alien to their traditions value system.

Discussions of the Findings

There were some significant differences between the responses of the three religious groups within the sample. For example, there was a tendency for the Sikh respondents to be less religious than their counterparts. For the majority of the Muslim respondents, the fathers were the most religious members of the family. It was Muslim women who became more religious after arriving at university, as compared to the Hindu and Sikh women. Again it was a notable minority of Muslim respondents that wanted single sex schooling and not the Hindu or Sikh women. Furthermore, it was a highly significant minority of Muslim women who favoured separate religious schools as opposed to a very small Hindu and Sikh minority. Many of the Muslim sample that wanted school uniform to be modified for religious reasons. It was found that more Sikh students used their mother tongue at university compared to Hindu and Muslim students. A majority of the Muslim women students who were not satisfied with the level of religious education given in schools. Many Sikh respondents that wanted sex education taught in schools, whereas a significant minority of Muslim respondents wanted sex education optional. A greater number of the Muslim respondents wanted Asian dishes on the school menus as compared to Sikh and Hindu respondents. The Muslim women students had been encouraged by a matriarchal member of the family whereas the Hindu and Sikh women were mainly encouraged by their fathers.

However, on certain issues there were no significant differences between the three religious groups, although, they held resolute views on these issues. For example, the majority of the Asian university women sample wanted school children to wear school uniform. They also wanted sex education and Asian topics to be taught whether they were compulsory or optional. The majority wanted to see more Asian teachers in schools and more Asian lecturers in universities.

Conclusion

It must, therefore be appreciated that South-East Asian girls are not a homogenous group, as perceived by ethnocentric British establishments and institutions. They are distinguishable, for example, by religion, sect, linguistic association, caste and country of origin. These findings suggest that there is a relationship between religious background and the variance in attitudes of Asian women undergraduates towards school education. Although there are commonalties between the three religious groups studied (i.e. Hindus, Muslims and Sikhs), there are also differences that were evident in some of the responses in the study which were influenced by religion.

All institutions, schools, colleges of further education, and higher education institutions need to understand the complexity of a group of students often just teamed 'Asian'. If they fail to understand the dissimilar effects of religion on minority ethnic students, the South-East Asian students will experience a degree of 'creedism' and lack of support due to the non-religious aligned separations. At the same time, the individuality of every student needs to be acknowledged. For instance, some students may interpret their membership of a religious group in a fundamentalist way while often others from the same religious group may be adapting their religious practices reflecting their membership of 'British' communities.

These complexities point very clearly to need for well thought out staff development policies for all education institutions. For instance, multiculturalism cannot be 'done' in one session that outlines the key principles and practices of different religions. At the same time staff, both academic and administrative, at all levels such as admissions, teaching, assessment, and career advice need to be involved.

Challenging stereotypes is an on-going, process of staff development recognising the different factors that affect the capabilities, beliefs, and needs of any given individual.

Bibliography

Basit, T.N. (1995), *Educational, Social and Career Aspirations of Teenage Muslim Girls in Britain: An Ethnographic Case Study*, Unpublished Ph.D. Thesis, University of Cambridge.

Cohen, L. and Manion, L. (1994), *Research Methods in Education*, Routledge, London.

Commission for Racial Equality, (1985), *Swann Report: A Response*, CRE, London.

Dhamsana, L. (1994), 'Asian Parents, Perceptions and Experiences about Inner City Schools - a Local Perspective', in *Multicultural Teaching*, Vol.12, No. 2, pp. 24-8.

Drury, B. (1991), 'Sikh Girls and the Maintenance of an Ethnic Culture'; in *New Community*, Vol. 7, No. 3, pp 387-399.

Ghuman, P.A.S. (1991), 'Have they Passed the Cricket Test? A Qualitative Study of Asian Adolescents', *Journal of Multilingual and Multicultural Development*, vol. 12, No5, pp.327-346.

Ghuman, P.A.S. (1994), *Coping with Two Cultures: A Study of British Asians and Indo-Canadian Adolescents*, Multilingual Matters, Clevedon.

Haw, K.F. (1994), 'Muslim Girls Schools, a conflict of Interest?', in *Gender and Education*, vol. 6, no.1.

Jackson, R. A. and Nesbitt, E. (1994), *Hindu Children in Britain*, Trentham Books, Stoke-on-Trent, UK.

Jacobson, J. (1997), 'Religion and Ethnicity: Dual and Alternative Sources of Identity among Young British Pakistanis', in *Ethnic and Racial Studies*, vol. 20, no.2, pp. 238-256.

McDermott, M. and Ahsan, M. (1986), *The Muslim Guide*, Islamic Foundation, London.

Modood, T. and Shiner, M. (1994), *Ethnic Minorities and Higher Education: Why are there Different rates of Entry?*, Policy Studies Institute, London.

Naipaul, V.S. (1982), *Islamic Journey*, Harmondsworth: Penguin, London.

Parker-Jenkins, M. (1991), 'Muslim Matters: the Educational Needs of the Muslim Child', in *New Community*, vol. 17, no.4, pp. 569-582.

Siann, G. and Khalid, R. (1984), 'Muslim Traditions and Attitudes to Female Education', in *Journal of Adolescence*, vol.7, pp.191-200.

Singh-Raud, H.(1997a), *Educational Attitudes and Aspirations of Asian Girls*, Unpublished Ph.D. Thesis, Manchester Metropolitan University, UK.

Singh-Raud, H.(1997b), *Educating Sita: The Education of British Asian Girls*, paper given at the British Educational Research Association Conference, September, York, England.

Singh, R. (1990), 'Ethnic Minority Experience in Higher Education', in *Higher Education Quarterly*, vol. 44, pp. 344-359.

Siegel, S. (1956), *Non-Parametric Statistis for the Behavioural Sciences*, McGraw-Hill, New York.

Skinner, G. (1990), 'Religion, Culture and Education', in Pumfrey, P. D. and Verma G.K. (eds.), *Race Relations and Urban Education*, Falmer, London.

Taylor, P. (1993), 'Minority Ethnic Groups and Gender in Access to Higher Education', in *New Community*, vol. 19, No.3, pp. 425-440.

Tomlinson, S. (1983), 'Black Women in Higher Education - Case Studies of University Women in Britain', in Barton, L. and Walker, S. (eds.), *Race, Class and Education*, Croom Helm, Beckenham.

Verma, G.K., Zec P. and Skinner, G. (1994), *The Ethnic Crucible: Harmony and Hostility in Multi-Ethnic Schools*, Falmer Press, London.

Woodrow, D. (1996), 'Cultural Inclinations Towards Studying Mathematics, and Sciences', in *New Community*, vol. 22, no.1, pp. 23-38.

5 Sins of Omission: Teacher Education and Race

RUSSELL JONES

Abstract

Currently 'race equality issues' barely feature at a national policy level. There is little evidence of what this lack of engagement has meant at the chalk face of initial teacher education. Whereas issues such as 'race' were often raised as part of the syllabus within traditional Sociology of Education courses, the present 'de-racialised discourse' has taken place alongside greater central government control over the content of teacher education over the last decade, pushing such issues onto the periphery. As we enter the new millennium, it seems as though for many newly qualified teachers equality issues are generally no longer relevant. In predominantly white areas of the country, where multicultural and anti-racist issues are all too easily marginalised. The lack of any clear direction at national level has meant that such issues are seen to be irrelevant to effective education.

In this chapter the focus is on a recent study undertaken by the author which demonstrates how so-called 'effective' training can produce teachers who have little knowledge, understanding or commitment with regard to our culturally diverse society. This clearly points to challenges not just for the traditional teacher education institutions, but schools which have been playing an increasingly greater role in the education of teachers. There is little evidence that partnership, mentoring, and improving effective, schooling have taken on board the significance of the student teachers understanding the nature and consequences of racism, the way children develop their attitudes and behaviour to people of different cultures, and the impact of race relations in the community on both the teachers and the children. The big question raised at the end of the chapter is how the curriculum for teacher education can take on the challenge of informing the student teachers about racism, preparing them to teach the children about dealing with racism, and at the same time giving support and space for the student teachers themselves to recognise and control their own racism.

Introduction

> Recent upheavals in the state education system have adopted a de-racialised discourse that has all but obliterated race equality issues at the national policy level.

The above statement by Gilborn (1996, p.175) underlines that 'race equality issues' barely feature at a national policy level. There is, however, little evidence of what this lack of engagement has meant at the chalk face of initial teacher education (ITE). Whereas issues such as 'race' were often raised as part of the syllabus within traditional Sociology of Education courses, the 'de-racialised discourse' suggested by Gillborn (1996) has developed alongside intervention into teacher training and education over the last decade, pushing such issues into a marginalised position which is barely perceptible in some programmes of ITE. As we enter the new millennium, it seems as though many beginning teachers feel that equality issues are largely the language of the past. In predominantly white areas of the country, where multicultural and antiracist issues are all too easily marginalised, the lack of any concerted direction at a national level has meant that there are even more excuses to claim that such issues are irrelevant, outdated and meaningless.

The Research Project

As the students who are currently being trained in institutions throughout the country will be the next generation of teachers for the new millennium, research was undertaken by the author (Jones, 1999) for a PhD to examine what beginning primary teachers in the predominantly white areas of the country actually learn about 'race' during the course of their training. In choosing this area, the shift towards school-based training for primary teachers was clearly important. Having been part of a mentor training programme whilst working as a Deputy Head, the researcher was already aware of the potential for non-National Curriculum subjects to become further marginalised in the drive towards a model of teacher education which devalued university-based theory in favour of the less critical and more practical chalk-face experience of the primary classroom. Issues of equality were not part of the training brief handed out as a package from schools. Neither were they identified as features of university modules. It seemed that the 'de-racialised discourse' proposed by Gillborn (1996) had already become an identifiable feature of programmes of ITE. Two groups of students from two separate providers of ITE, each offering PGCE courses in primary education, were studied. One provided a school-based model of training, the second a more traditional, university-based model. The combined programmes offered teaching experience over three counties using schools where there were predominantly, if not exclusively, white children typically in a rural or semi-rural setting. All students on both courses were white, there were no ethnic minority lecturers on either university programme, and there were no ethnic minority teachers or mentors in the schools used for training purposes.

The research methodology included watching the students learn their craft, collecting of course documentation, attending of relevant lectures, workshops and field trips and interviewing course leaders, tutors, head teachers, supervisory teachers, and mentors at all stages of the training. By asking for volunteers the researcher was able to select a sample of ten students from each course and trace their progress through their entire course of training. This included regular semi-structured interviews using open ended questions, beginning in the induction weeks and working through to a final interview during the last ten days of the course. Each student interview was taped, transcribed in full and returned for respondent validity. The researcher also arranged to teach alongside each student wherever possible at some point in their training to include some level of participant observation. 24 schools were listed over the three counties and in total 157 formal interviews (107 with students, 32 with supervising teachers, mentors and head teachers and 18 with University staff) were conducted.

It became immediately apparent that the universities were over-reliant on 'permeation' as a teaching strategy, and that the overriding response to the issue from the perspective of the students was that of 'colourblindness'. Both of these terms need to be explored in some detail in order to contextualise some of the responses and experiences discussed later in this chapter.

'Permeation' was a term which was regularly used by university staff when discussing ways in which they approached issues of equality and race in particular. The Swann Report expressed concern that permeation could be 'just a paper promise' (Great Britain, 1985), and Gaine (1988) warned of the danger that 'things can become so well permeated that they disappear altogether'. Ten years ago it was argued that 'permeation as a model for change cannot work whilst it is being 'implemented' by people who have not raised their own conscious understanding of issues of race and racism (ARTEN, 1988). Despite these concerns, there was a clear expectation at the universities that these issues would 'permeate through the entire curriculum', yet when subject lecturers were questioned about the ways in which multicultural education and equal opportunities were covered on the courses the reply was that there simply was insufficient time available to cover these issues. Typically, lecturers pointed to materials and lesson plans which once brought equality issues into their teaching, but when questioned further they replied that their current syllabus had been rationalised in some way and that these lessons were amongst those which had been cut in order to maintain an acceptable core content. Even after elaborating on their timetable constraints, these lecturers remained convinced that their colleagues still managed to incorporate equality issues within *their* teaching. Occasionally, when specific examples of positive practice were given, the lecturer(s) in question also revealed that they too had had to rationalise their modules to meet new criteria and that they no longer found time to cover equality issues. Typical responses to this line of questioning included:

> We haven't even talked about it and I think that is a pity that we don't, I suppose I just hope that my colleagues portray the same kind of feel about teaching. But that's an assumption isn't it?
> (Lecturer on university-based course).

Lecturer 1: The ideal thing would be that it permeates the curriculum area, but the issue should be something that (pause) you know (pause) it should be focused on specifically as an explicit element within the course...
(Lecturer on university-based course).

Researcher: You said that there are other areas of the curriculum where you know that multicultural education is a feature...

Lecturer 1: I don't know how much (pause) in all honesty I don't know how much it is emphasised...
(Lecturer on university-based course).

Researcher: Is there any time when everyone gets together and talks about things like multicultural education?

Lecturer 2: No.
(Lecturer on school-based course).

Equality issues would permeate through some form of osmosis through teacher education courses, but there were some lecturers who recognised that this was unlikely, and then felt frustrated at the lack of opportunity to incorporate equality issues within their teaching programmes. These lecturers often felt isolated in their beliefs and unable to articulate their concerns as issues such as inspection and assessment always took priority. These lecturers each told me that their commitment to equality issues was the result of personal experience, and had little or nothing to do with the professional development of the institution:

> Researcher: So all the things that you have learnt about race are to do with you as a professional rather than say staff development here or...
>
> Lecturer 3: Oh God yes (laughs).
> (Lecturer on university-based course).
>
> Researcher: It's all to do with your experiences as a teacher?
>
> Lecturer 3: (laughs). It's *nothing* to do with what I've experienced here. Sadly. Nothing.
> (Lecturer on university-based course).
>
> Researcher: How do you think multicultural education is co-ordinated across the faculty?
>
> Lecturer 4: It isn't.
> (Lecturer on university-based course).

If multicultural education was not a feature of the training at the universities, it certainly was not a feature in the classrooms in which the beginning teachers were trained. When asked about the ways in which these issues were covered in schools, supervising teachers and mentors said:

> There is nothing to address, really. Nothing at all...The tendency on teaching practice is you address things as they arise don't you? You say 'What do I do in this situation?' and you address it like that, so it's just not there.
> (Mentor on school-based course).

It's the job of the college. They've got enough staff, it's their job. Let's be honest here, who's getting their training done on the cheap? It's their job. I have never dealt with things liked multicultural education with a student. It's not really an issue here anyway but it's the college who should be doing it.
(Supervising teacher on university-based course).

It was becoming increasingly difficult to identify the ways in which equality issues *did* feature as part of teacher education programmes.

Clearly the university lecturers felt themselves under curricular constraints which had marginalised equal opportunities elements of their teaching out of existence. Classroom teachers and mentors felt that it was entirely inappropriate for them to deal with these issues when they had the more pressing responsibility of introducing these young people to the classroom, and facilitating those first fumbling steps into the teaching profession. If universities were finding it increasingly difficult to locate space to incorporate issues of equality on their initial teacher education courses, and the schools in which students were trained did not see this as part of their training responsibility, then there was little chance of beginning teachers training in predominantly white classrooms coming to develop a critical understanding about social issues such as ethnicity during the course of their training. These findings resonate clearly with Gillborn's (1996) concerns, and Gollnick's (1992, p.238) claim that:

Research is needed on how to prepare whites, who make up 90 per cent of the teacher candidates ... , to work effectively in communities that are culturally different than their own. Can we teach candidates to recognise and overcome their own biases?

Whilst teaching students to 'recognise and overcome their own biases' is a problematic aim, if not one that is philosophically impossible, the point should certainly be made that beginning teachers need work on identifying the ways in which their own prejudices operate. They also need to realize that their biases sometimes do not translate comfortably into classrooms which contain cultures that are significantly different to those of the students. Whereas this is a wider issue for teacher educators in general, it is a more pressing and even more difficult problem in exclusively white classrooms as we reach the millennium, where beginning teachers are even less likely to have teaching and learning experiences that will bring their own prejudices and biases into the foreground.

Having established that the equality issues input on the initial teacher education programmes studied was minimal at best, it was less than surprising to find that the students on these programmes adopted a position of 'colourblindness' to deal with the specific issue of race. Put simply, this is a (non) strategy of conceptualising the issue of race; by ignoring it completely. It is only too easy to see the ways in which students can be attracted to this stance in the all white primary school.

To begin with, there is the 'No Problem Here' syndrome (Gaine, 1988), whereby race is casually dismissed as an issue because there are no ethnic minority children in the school. Secondly, there is the training issue, where the priority for students, their mentors and supervising thatteachers is clearly located in planning, lesson delivery, assessment, recording and reporting. From the author's personal experience and from the study undertaken it is clear that issues such as equal opportunities are often very low on the list of priorities for all concerned on a PGCE course, but in an all white primary school, 'race' can be even less of an issue. Thirdly, primary educators often refer to themselves as members of the 'school family' and the close professional and social relationships develop within small primary schools is unlikely to encourage critical social analysis from students. The model is more likely to be one of showing the student how to become part of that school family. This also means that PGCE students in small, rural, all white primary schools are likely to adopt positions of 'strategic compliance' (Sparkes and Mackay, 1996) whereby they do not want to 'rock the boat' on school experience, and instead follow the models of teaching they are offered, replicating them, safe in the knowledge that they are more likely to succeed when their final assessment comes around. In a similar vein, one study (Hodgkinson, 1992), into student roles and personal relationships during primary school teaching practices recognised that 'personality characteristics can become highly significant' again suggesting that classroom performance factors can become less important than 'fitting in'. The findings of the research reported in this chapter would support this belief, and concur with much of the valuable work done in this area by Edwards and Collison (1995), suggesting that the process of 'fitting in' sometimes precludes the kinds of critical professional discourses that would be desirable between mentor and beginning teacher in favour of developing a supportive, familial relationship more reminiscent of parent/child roles.

All these elements were discernible within the kinds of response the researcher was given by students working in schools, and they were contributory factors in the ways in which they saw themselves developing as practitioners. These students tended to perceive race as an area that simply did not need to addressed. Issues such as race, gender and class were often seen as problems of the past, issues which had long since been resolved and now largely redundant in the context of their training. It is important to remember that these (white) students typically came from professional backgrounds in predominantly white areas of the country, their models of teaching and lecturing were exclusively white, and they were working in predominantly (and in some cases exclusively) white primary schools. This was acknowledged in interview by one of the course leaders at the university:

> We attract a fairly white, middle class, Protestant type ... most people have got some church background, they've got an interest in children that shows itself in either Sunday school teaching or brownies or guides ... I think that we tend to attract people from a similar kind of background, fairly small town or village background. So we end up attracting a type of person who could be closed minded, in particular could be closed minded in terms of equal opportunities.

The present research would largely support this stereotype, but would also indicate that that there were few reasons to believe that neither the schools nor the universities provided any kind of 'revelatory' experience would change any of their opinions about issues of equality in general, and certainly nothing to alter any of their views about race. When students were questioned as part of this study, they demonstrated an understanding that relied heavily on 'colourblindness', and on a vague notion of perceiving the children as individuals and treating everyone the same'. During the initial round of interviews typical responses were:

> As far as I am concerned they are all children, they're not girls and boys...a child is a child, it doesn't matter what sex they are or what colour they are, what religion...
> (Beginning teacher on university-based course).

> They are individuals. I don't look at them as brown or white, or boys and girls, it's how they are as a class. Their personalities...
> (Beginning teacher on school-based course).

> I think it is better to have relationships with the children in your class because they are individuals, they are not Tommy who's black, Billy who's in a wheelchair, they are Tommy and Billy and the wheelchair and the colour bit doesn't even come close. It's more

about what is going on here (indicates her heart) that I am interested in, and I get very cross with people who start treating them in different ways because of that, whether they mean to or not. It makes me very angry.

(Beginning teacher on university-based course).

These statements highlight just how complicated the apparently simplistic notions of identity and individuality can be. In adjacent sentences the third respondent illustrates the oversimplification of this approach by intending to conceptualise the children in her care as individuals, yet then states that she did not want to recognise their colour or their sex. She revolved by then intimating that she wanted to suppress their individuality in order to see them as 'a class'. The problem revolved yet again when she finally qualified her argument with another appeal to the value of their individual personalities. Her naive desire to treat children as individuals simply equates with 'treating them all the same'. This in turn equated with the notion that it is somehow admirable or desirable that the teacher should ignore the fact that Tommy is black despite the reality that every child in the class can see that he is black, or that the teacher should ignore Billy's wheelchair despite the reality that every child in the classroom can see he is unable to move around the room without it. It would seem as though the concept of child here becomes the exact opposite of 'individual' and instead becomes a category. Whilst wanting to maintain the sense of the child as an individual, these students demonstrated willingness to categorise them in a homogeneous group labelled 'the child' where even skin colour or disability can be conceptually disregarded. Clearly this is a difficult starting point when attempting to explore issues of ethnic identity.

In order to explore more fully the whole business of 'colourblindness' and its part within a 'de-racialised discourse', it is relevant to repeat a story noted in the research which begins to suggest that there is a long way to go before it can be assumed that equality issues will play a significant part in initial teacher education for the millennium. Whilst the vast majority of the students in the study were placed in primary schools where there were no ethnic minority children at all, a couple of students were placed in schools where the ethnic minority population of the school amounted to two or three children per class. Helen was one of these students. Over the course of the day the researcher had negotiated interviews with both Helen and her mentor, and arranged to spend the afternoon team teaching in Helen's classroom. The researcher stumbled across a racial attack (discussed in more detail in Jones, 1999). No teacher saw it happen, but some forty or so children were witness to the incident. In order to explore further how such incidents happen, the researcher decided to revisit the school as soon as possible. In the meantime, he constructed a 'fictional' scenario that described the attack he had seen. The intention was twofold. Firstly it would allow the researcher to present it during interviews as a purely speculative account and invite school members to comment on what might happen should the incident have taken place in their school. Secondly it was sufficiently detailed to not withstand any attempt at pretence should the scenario be recognised. This would then allow time to see if any of the forty or so children who had witnessed the attack had reported it to the teachers.

At no stage during any of the subsequent interviews did any respondent suggest that the incident was in fact real. In interview, Helen's mentor said that she had spent her entire career in the same school, which she regularly described as being 'happy'. She stated also that she had received no training before being asked to supervise students. This was interesting as the researcher had been told by the university that this teacher was one of the best practitioners available to them. She was held in such high regard that typically she was used to recapture students who were in danger of failing, or who had had particularly unsuccessful first school attachments. During the interview she said that when she first came to the school there were no ethnic minority children at all; when she came thirty-two years ago. They had one little West Indian boy who used to sit in the nursery and cry because 'Why wasn't anybody like he was?'. She stated that there was no multicultural policy or statement in the school, but that they were 'looking towards writing one'.

During the interview in reference to the equal opportunities provision made by her university, Helen said that she found that the discussion of race and multicultural issues at the university:

> ...didn't tell me anything I didn't already know. I think if you are already sensitive to the issues then (pause) you know, ... preaching to the converted really.

Helen confirmed this in a later interview when she said:

> We just seemed to be talking about things that we knew already, ... didn't seem to be really going anywhere, just confirming things we were already aware of.

Neither Helen nor her mentor was able to point the researcher in the direction of a multicultural policy within the school. The headteacher confirmed that a multicultural policy for the school did not exist, that there was no agreed method of dealing with racial incidents, and that the school was not really 'party to these things':

> No, I haven't got one, and I don't think we (pause) I don't think (pause) it is one of the many policies that I haven't got and we should have. I think that equal opportunities covers that.

Whilst it cannot be argued that existence of a multicultural policy with a school necessarily equates with positive practice, it is an indicator that at least the issue has been discussed in some form. It is important to remember here the findings of the MacDonald Inquiry (Burnage, 1989). One of the conclusions was that it was clear that any antiracist policy would be totally ineffective if carried out in a vacuum. Policies which have been 'grafted-on' can 'easily lead to a marginalisation' whereby non-involved staff are able to see themselves as exempt from the responsibility of dealing with these issues.

With Helen's school, however, not even a 'grafted-on' policy existed. There are still schools where no such discussion has taken place, no such documentation exists there and that the predominantly (or exclusively) white rural primary school is likely to be an example of this in practice. Of the twenty three schools used in this study, the researcher was unable to locate a single policy statement on multicultural education, or on 'race' issues within the school. One infant school offered their documentation but as the research was about the way beginning teachers are trained in Key Stage 2, their evidence could not be included in the findings. It is possible that some schools did have the relevant documentation but were not prepared to let outsiders read. It was clear that multicultural education did not form part of an open, ongoing dialogue between head teachers, mentors, teachers and students at any point during their training.

When Helen was eventually presented with the 'fictional' story and asked what she thought would happen if the incident had happened in her school, her reply was:

> Well, I would expect that both parties would be taken into the Head, and each to give their side of the story and (pause) it's the same old question. What do you say? (silence).

Remembering that at least one and probably two entire classes had witnessed the incident she was asked if the children in her school were the sort who would want to tell their teacher if they saw such an incident happening. Helen said:

Yes, they would want to tell...I think that by and large they are good children.

In her final interview, when it was explained that it had actually happened outside her classroom door, Helen seemed reluctant to discuss the incident or to make any direct comment on it, but said:

You feel so helpless though...the cleaner at our school, the top one, she said something about 'Oh Pakis, I can't be doing with them'. I didn't know what to say...the cleaner in my classroom said 'Oh isn't she terrible, Helen?' in a jokey sort of way but it's such a contentious issue and if I said 'I'm sorry I don't agree with that...' (pause) I'm ashamed that I didn't.

The headteacher was also given the story of the attack as a fictional scenario and asked for her comments should this kind of incident happen in her school. She told me:

I mean I touch wood when I say this but at the moment that isn't an issue at the school. There has been within the last three months an issue developing outside the school, not with *our* children, with the *older* children, with teenagers...there have been quite a lot of disturbances at nights. That I think might well (pause) I think in twelve months, two years time, that it could well work it's way down (original emphasis).

The headteacher stated that the staff were all aware of these incidents. It is, therefore, interesting to note that even though they had been informed of the 'disturbances', there was still no indication that anyone felt it was a matter of some urgency, or that the school needed to agree a positive policy in this area or that it was an issue that needed to be discussed with the children.

Helen later said:

I have never heard anything said or got any vibes off the children. Whether that's different in Year Five and Year Six I don't know. I did notice the other morning when I was walking to school on the wall it was spray painted 'Pakis out'.

At this point it is possible to see how 'colourblindness' impacts on a school's community. Helen's school was one which contained an ethnic minority of some 6 per cent. These children were subject to attacks in their own school, ritual verbal abuse in their own classrooms (as outlined by Helen), racist graffiti outside the school buildings and racial violence in their community in the evenings. The school's response to these children's realities was to be 'colourblind'. Having taught in the school, and having witnessed some of the ways in which these children suffered, Helen remained unable to conceive of any alternative strategy. When Helen was interviewed at the end of her training she still felt as though she would not want to move away from a 'colourblind' approach, stating that:

> I still feel that by bringing it to the fore you can put focus on the child and it can easily lead to them feeling more isolated.

The need to bring beginning teachers to a point where they recognise and challenge the social and cultural biases they bring with them to the course has been well documented (Eggleston, 1993), and there are particular resonances for those trained in exclusively white contexts who go on to teach in inner city areas. According to Siraj-Blatchford (1993, p.33):

> Students must be taught the importance of sharing the community of the child, as too many inner-city teachers come in from outside and never really perceive the needs of the community group, they impose their own values and education... White students need to understand the 'black experience', and this should not be interpreted or taught as a cultural or ethnic experience; they need to understand the realities of the day-to-day lives of black people living within the confines of white social practices, norms and structures.

The recent joint Teacher Training Agency/Commission for Racial Equality Report (1998) intended to look at the ways in which teachers are prepared to teach in a multicultural society quite rightly focuses on recruitment and retention of ethnic minority teachers and the particular needs of ethnic minority pupils in schools. Whilst there is a reference that 'All teachers need to be well-prepared to work in multi-ethnic classrooms', there is no indication that there are particular problems related to the training of teachers in predominantly white areas of the country. This is all the more disappointing since the evidence from this study was submitted to the conference that prepared the report and subsequent action plan.

Conclusion

It is clear that beginning teachers such as Helen, in their predominantly white primary schools, remain unlikely to be prepared to work in culturally diverse classrooms, and that their personal prejudices and biases are often left unchallenged through the exclusively white context in which they have been trained. If the new millennium is to see a reappraisal of 'equality issues' then there are several areas where significant starting points could be made.

Permeation as a vehicle for multicultural education simply does not work. The present research would suggest that the providers of initial teacher education still hold the belief that permeation is a successful strategy when the reality is that this simply is not the case. For equality issues to become part of ITE in the new millennium, providers need to have the courage to place compulsory equal opportunities sessions firmly on their course outlines. If permeation is expected to be a feature of ITE provision, then it cannot be left to chance; modules need to be developed to see exactly where this happens, what form it takes, what students are expected to learn through these processes, and how this is being evaluated on an ongoing basis.

Providers of ITE in predominantly white areas of the country need to be mindful of the social backgrounds of their student population and the schools used for training purposes. This research would suggest that school-based training and the resultant student-mentor relationships in comfortable, rural surroundings are unlikely to raise some of the equality issues which beginning teachers need to think carefully about in order to become rounded professionals.

There are particular professional issues about the nature of the relationship between the student and the mentor in the small, rural, all-white primary school (particularly on long term placements) that need to be further explored before it can be presumed that schoolshave either the facility or the inclination to want to address equality issues as part of their long term training brief.

ITE institutions need the support of different government agencies so that schools that undertake education of student teachers, and newly qualified teachers on their staff have similar approaches to equality issues. The institutions cannot force the schools to adopt any particular policies. Especially in rural areas where there are likely to limited places in schools for students,, they may be under pressure to use every school that is available, regardless of any shortcomings on equality issues.

The widely held reliance on 'colourblindness' needs to be held up to closer scrutiny at some point in the ITE process. Students need to realise that 'colourblindness' does not result in equality of education provision and experience. Similarly, students need to be given some opportunity to explore their own reactions to overt racism in schools, as too many expressed a sense of 'helplessness' and 'inadequacy'.

Providers of ITE working with school partners need to realise that schools in predominantly white areas of the country often find it difficult to handle issues such as multicultural education. Schools are sometimes reluctant to deal with 'race' issues through fear of 'creating a problem' and generating an adverse reputation in an educational market place. It is, therefore, all the more important that providers of ITE courses accept the mantle for this aspect of teacher training in order to ensure that students have meaningful understanding of equality issues.

Bibliography

Anti-Racist Teacher Education Network (eds) (1988), *Anti-racist Teacher Education, Permeation: The Road to Nowhere*, Jordanhill College of Education, Glasgow, UK.
Burnage Report (1989), *Murder in the Playground: The Report of the MacDonald Inquiry into Racism and Racial Violence in Manchester Schools*, Longsigh Press, London.
Edwards, A. and Collison, J. (1995), 'What do Teacher Mentors tell Student Teachers about Pupil Learning in Infant Schools?', *Teachers and Teaching: Theory and Practice*, Vol.1, No.2, pp. 265-280.
Eggleston, J. (1993), 'Educating Teachers to Combat Equality', Verma, G. (ed). *Inequality and Teacher Education*, Falmer Press, London.
Gaine, C. (1987), *No Problem Here*, Hutchinson, London.
Gillborn, D., (1996), 'Student Roles and Perspectives in Antiracist Education: A Crisis of White Ethnicity?', *British Education Research Journal*, vol.22, No. 2, pp.165-179.
Gollnick, D.M. (1992), 'Multicultural Education: Policies and Practices', in Grant, C.A. (ed), *Teacher Education in Research and Multicultural Education*, Falmer, London, pp. 218-259.
Great Britain, Department of Education and Science (1985), *Education For All*, HMSO, London.
Hodgkinson, K. (1992), *A Study of Student Roles and Personal Relationships During Primary School Teaching Practice*, Department of Education, Loughborough University, UK.
Jones, R. (1998), *Deafening Silence: Telling Stories of Beginning Teachers' Understanding of Ethnicity*, PhD Thesis, Manchester Metropolitan University, UK.
Jones, R. (1999), *Teaching Racism or Tackling it?: Multicultural Stories from White Beginning Teachers*, Trentham Books, Stoke-On-Trent, UK.
Siraj-Blatchford, I. (1993), 'Racial Equality and Effective Teacher Education' in *'Race,' Gender and the Education of Teachers*, Open University Press, Buckingham, UK.

Sparkes, A.C. and MacKay, R. (1996), Teaching Practice and the Micropolitics of Self Presentation, in *Pedagogy in Practice*, Vol.2, No.1. p .3

Teacher Training Agency/Commission for Racial Equality (1998), *Teaching in Multi-Ethnic Britain: A Joint Report by the Teacher Training Agency and the Commission for Racial Equality*, TTA/CRE, London.

6 The Reality of Isolation for Black Student Teachers

SUE LEWIS

Abstract

In the last chapter Russell Jones outlined the lack of commitment among teacher education institutions to effective implementation of equality policies. He was focusing particularly on institutions in what have been normally called white areas. However, this lack of commitment in teacher education institutions is also of concern in relation to experiences of black and minority ethnic students.

There is literature that clearly details the disturbing experiences of isolated black and ethnic minority children in schools, and the general racism experienced by black and minority ethnic students in higher education. Recent focus on experiences of teacher education students has also highlighted the difficulties they additionally face in their teaching experience situation

In this chapter the knowledge of the experiences of two students alerts us to the type of experiences black and minority ethnic students are likely to undergo, especially when they are isolated. Educators need to understand the totality of the life experiences of the students, not just when they are on the campus. The need to learn and understand the experiences of even a small number of students is justified on how greatly they can demonstrate to the educationalists the tensions and the traumas the students can go through.

Individual students could be trying to work out how they handle discrimination, when little support is available from other people. Helping the students in this process needs to be an essential part of their education, apart from helping them to qualify as teachers. This is an example of a strategy that could be more relevant than the provision of black student support groups.

Introduction

Recently Siraj-Blatchford ((1993, p.92) wrote:

> It is disturbing that ... many higher education institutions do not feel the need to promote equality policies and practice. Their complacency may be due to the fact that they do not perceive themselves as capable of unequal treatment or perhaps it is assumed that the liberal culture of higher education is in some way unable to foster and perpetuate discrimination ... it is vital that ... we listen to what our black and female students articulate about their experiences.

Seven years further on, as we enter the new millennium, teacher educators are still not listening hard enough and their complacency is still ill-founded. This chapter contains extracts from stories illustrating 'one side of the coin', the views of two black education students concerning their experiences while at university. Although they provide only a microscopic image within the big picture, they raise the question whether any progress has been made, at least within the institution where these two individuals studied.

The focus is the life-history research of the very few black students on Initial Teacher Education (ITE) courses in a rural faculty of a large metropolitan university in the North West of England (UNW), where the author lectures in Secondary Education. A number of people and events have influenced the choice of research focus and the methodology but, perhaps central has been the experience of marrying a West Indian and living with him in the white highlands of North Wales and Cheshire. Significant also was the meeting with a student of African origin at UNW who had decided to write about his experiences on school placement for his final assignment. Through this piece of writing, he began to explore his own understanding of what it meant to be black and a teacher. Witnessing this process of self-discovery led the author to the realisation that here was a story to explore first hand. Moreover, it soon became clear that he, like half of the other six respondents, was fostered/adopted by white parents. This may/may not be significant with respect to their choice of a white rural college for their ITE course. Each of the respondents was male and usually in the position of being the only black/ethnic minority student in his year. Five were Afro-Caribbean, one was Asian.

This chapter will focus on incidents taken from a series of hour-long interviews with two respondents. The young men were training to be PE teachers, both from the south of England. One was Asian and grew up in London - with his birth family, the other was Afro-Caribbean and was adopted into an upper middle class white family as a toddler. The incidents described took place over the previous twelve months.

Shaban's Story - Third Year

In the academic year of 1995/1996 Shaban came into the third year class for professional studies. He appeared to be a lively and committed student who took every opportunity to write about aspects of multicultural/antiracist interaction and frequently commented that he had not thought of racism as an issue while growing up in London. It had only become important to him, he insisted, since coming to university where concerns about the multicultural nature of society were significant by their absence from the curriculum.

During the year two incidents occurred over which he felt he had to take a stand. Both were with members of the PE staff and both involved comments which were meant to be jokes but which Shaban found offensive. It is interesting that in both instances Shaban felt strongly, and strong enough to confront the lecturers concerned. The first situation was sorted out amicably after a lengthy discussion where the lecturer apologised and accepted that he had been insensitive.

The second incident was not resolved so happily. The remark, concerning the number of 'dirty little foreigners coming over here to swamp our sports', was made in a public lecture. Shaban felt angry and upset that such a comment could be made by a member of staff. He followed the lecturer to his office and told him that he felt that such a statement/joke was inappropriate. The result was a heated argument with Shaban being ordered out of the room. The lecturer denied making the comment at all and other students Shaban talked to refused to get involved, saying that they hadn't heard the original comment. Shortly after this, Shaban received a bare pass for a piece of work on Racism in Sport, previously submitted to this same member of staff. This grade was significantly lower than marks Shaban was getting for other work and he felt, rightly or wrongly, that the incident had influenced his lecturer's attitude towards him and his work.

It was at this point that he came to discuss the matter with the author. However, when she approached the head of PE informally, she was told, 'It's Shaban, he's always complaining'. Bird (1996) regards such a response as far from untypical, pointing out that part of the difficulty is that the problems faced by black students are often not recognised and so nothing is done. He (Bird, 1996, p.2) suggested:

there are some tendencies to say that black students exaggerate their problems and/or that the problems they face are related exclusively to their own cultural values and attitude.

It is interesting to note, however, that Shaban's assignment was re-marked by a second member of staff and he was told to submit his work to one particular tutor only in future.

As time passed, Shaban became increasingly anxious, saying that he felt other students were making silly jokes for his benefit to indicate their support for the member of staff he had crossed. He began to feel isolated and even talked of leaving the course. He had been advised by the PE Department not to discuss any further incidents with the author in particular and was worried about the fact that he did come to talk. I decided, therefore, to seek advice from the Head of School. He was sympathetic, but it was agreed that a formal disciplinary proceeding was not the most positive way forward. It should be communicated to the PE Department that such comments and behaviour were unacceptable, and that this situation would be monitored. Should Shaban be victimised in any way, formal action would be the next step. Shaban seemed to be reassured to a degree and appeared to be regaining his enthusiasm for the course.

However, at the end of the academic year, when his parents came to pick him up for the summer, he suddenly announced that they were unhappy about the events during the year and he might, in fact, drop out of the course. The author's concern was partly that she had not supported him sufficiently well, and secondly, that the whole matter had highlighted the vulnerability of black students in particular and the micro-political consequence of setting Education against PE staff.

Shaban's Story - 4th Year

Shaban did return for the fourth year of his course, but adopted a different position. He distanced himself quite literally from the college by moving to a nearby town to stay with members of his extended family - a condition for his return, laid down by his parents. He only commuted into college a few days a week. In response to a question about the course generally and whether or not he'd enjoyed it, he answered:

> I think college has got a lot to offer, it's got good facilities in terms of the PE. Maybe, if there were a few more ethnic minority students, possibly (pause) you can relate to them. I've been brought

up in a multicultural you know, environment so (pause) you know, at times, yeah, you need someone to talk to and relate to.

Regarding strategies he had adopted in order to survive in the white highlands he commented:

> Being thick-skinned at times or laugh it off if there are any stupid comments, you know but I can't think of anything really malicious said towards my face. There's a few jokes but you laugh it off...

In other words, like the PGCE students interviewed by Maguire et al (1996) to get through the course, the students basically keep their mouths shut.

What is extraordinary, of course, is that previously, Shaban chose to open his mouth and suffered a great deal of anxiety as a result. He, too, appeared to have now decided that the priority was to pass the course. Indeed, he completed a very successful final school experience in a Catholic school in a large town and was highly commended by the external examiners. His concern in 1996/1997 (his final year) centred around whether he would get a job. He was working hard but debating whether he should apply to all white schools or not, as he wondered whether he could cope. His battles of the previous year were dismissed as follows:

> There was a number of things (pause) you know (pause) I mean like that comment that was made (pause) but, you know, you forget about those things, I've forgotten about it now and just get on.

He did, however, add an aside that he knew that a black member of the football team had been subjected to a lot of racial abuse - but the student had since left. Shaban added the following comment later on in the same interview:

> I wouldn't say I'm black (pause) I haven't got black ... (indecipherable) I've got olive skin but I also have a name which is not err (pause) is not a common name.

On the other hand, he had some very interesting thoughts on being a role model in terms of an Asian teacher:

> Author: Do you see yourself as being a role model for black kids in any way?

Shaban: Err (pause) I don't know (pause). Yeah, I'd like to think of myself as a role model but I'm not perfect, I wouldn't say I'm 100 per cent perfect and I err ... I'm a bit sceptical about the term 'role model' at times. Yeah. If I'm going to become labelled as a role model I feel like I've got to put (pause). I've got to analyse everything I'm doing and I think I've got to be perfect all the time, which I'm not. So having that tag, or that label is quite a difficult one to keep up with (pause). Yeah, I think it would be good (pause). I think I'd be a good role model.

Peter

The second story concerns Peter, a very articulate Afro-Caribbean young man who, again, was the only black student in his year. He was also studying PE but only in year three of the four year course. He had been adopted by an upper middle class white couple when he was very young and subsequently spent most of his school life at boarding school. He said he was used to being the only black person in an all white environment and appeared to be confident and happy to talk openly about his experience of education.

In an interview focusing on his college life, he mentioned three events which had caused him pain. The first involved a group of students, himself included, supporting another black student against a group of Sports Science undergraduates at a college disco. This, Peter felt, was dealt with successfully as the perpetrators were disciplined and banned from the bar. His own view was that they:

> were drunk, not too severely, I mean they'd had a few to drink but it was still no cause for saying what they said and doing what they did (pause) err and I would go with that sort of line of thinking for, you know, all the time.

The first incident where he was the target occurred one evening when he had gone to an Indian restaurant for a take-away. The restaurant was in the small town where his campus was located. A group of PE and Sports Science students happened to be in there, half way through their meal:

Peter: Again these two were drunk and some of the football team I get on very well with, er, you know. We go out quite a lot together and one of them is on my course (pause). He's the captain who's on my course and he said, you know, 'Hello, how are you doing?' and so on and then these two just piped up, er, with quite a few racist remarks and I was a bit stunned, you know. You don't expect it when you walk in there.

Author: Do you mind telling me what they said?

Peter: I don't mind telling you what they said (pause). First of all it was like, ohh a few strong words but they were saying, like, you know, 'Oh, the nigger's come in' and things like that. Er, er, a couple of, er, (pause) I can't remember all the comments but it was comments like that. Er, and I was (pause) I was on my own and I was just like, you know, 'What have I done?' ... (omission). The manager had heard it and he was like 'Are you OK?' and that sort of thing and I was just (pause) 'I'm fine' and 'Don't worry about it, I'll just get my food and go'... (omission) I said, you know, 'Don't worry about it, I'm only having a takeaway (pause) let them finish their meal', but there was a couple of other tables in there of just local people, not from college, and it was (pause) I feel bad for them personally because they were having a nice meal on whatever day it was and they didn't want to be there. You know. They asked to have their bill or their takeaway or whatever.

The manager asked the group of students to leave the restaurant but Peter intervened, explaining his response by saying:

and I feel (pause) I was so annoyed about it because they had come out for a nice meal and it's like his (meaning the manager's) business and so on, and just for the sake of these people. At the same time because I have had racism before in my life, er, I let it go by me, at the time, but I feel it ... (omission). When I got home and sort of you sit down and you sort of (pause) it hits you and it was (pause) it doesn't make me cry but it sort of makes me cry, you know, it makes me cry inside if you like, and I found it hard to get to sleep that night.

The second incident also took place off campus outside a club in a nearby town where Peter and some friends had gone for the evening. Peter was driving and had left the club first. While he was standing outside, another group of Sports Science/PE students appeared and began to shout abuse. They knew who he was because Peter commented that they had called his name. A third group of young people, not connected with the University, stopped to ask if he needed support. Peter assured them he was fine and was just waiting for his friends. These observers were so concerned, however, they actually reversed the car to where he was standing:

Peter: And sort of wound down the window and he was like saying, 'That guy's out of order', and I was saying, 'Yes, I know, but don't worry about it. I'm just waiting for my friends they'll be out in a moment'. I think one of them had come out at this stage or was in the doorway or something like this and I said, 'Look, there's one of them over there, I'll be fine'. And he was all ready to go and fight them on my behalf.

Author: Was he white this chap?

Peter: Yes (pause) and he had (pause) there were four of them in the car, of which two or three were lads, and he was like the older one, you know, he said, 'We'll sort them out for you, mate', and everything like that. And I said, 'No, it's OK'.

Author: Was he from College?

Peter: No, he wasn't from College. They were local people from ... Basically, I said, 'No, look honestly, I'll be fine' (pause) 'cause I could see one of the guys coming out and I said, 'Look, please don't cause any trouble', and I said to them, 'Look, I know the guy, he's from College, don't worry about it', so they drove off. And the others came

	out of the door and I walked over to them and said, 'We're leaving now!'.
Author:	Did you explain why?
Peter:	I didn't right there and then but they were like, 'What's going on?', but I just said, 'Get in the car, I need to leave now'. And then on the way back I told them what happened because I was quite abrupt with them and they're my friends. You know, they'd been having a really good evening and they wondered why I was so het up so it sort of (pause) they go from that happy, feel good, you know, as you do as you come out of a night club (pause) had a good night to trying to sober up and know what's going on sort of thing. You know, trying to control the situation and I said, 'Look, it doesn't matter just get in the car'.
Author:	Were you driving?
Peter:	Yes, I was driving. And, er, on the way back I told them so they were sort of, they understood where I was coming from, why I was being abrupt ...

One of the first things that was noticeable about both these episodes was Peter's apparent concern at the way people's evenings were spoilt by these scenes. He appeared to be taking it upon himself to 'rescue' the situation as far as possible, almost to be taking responsibility for the racism he experienced. This again resonates with Maguire et al's (1996) findings that black students employed tactics such as keeping quiet, and taking the blame for misunderstandings. It is significant that Peter did not discuss what had happened with any member of staff even though the situation has still not been resolved. He commented on how difficult it was, as he saw these students around in college all the time. He eventually told the author. Bird (1996, p.5) points out that:

> it is, of course, still an interesting point that, for many black students, the research environment is the one in which issues of race and discrimination are first being discussed.

Conclusion

These stories have highlighted a number of issues. Firstly, the few black students on ITE courses at UNW often feel very vulnerable and isolated. There are no obvious support structures in place. Bird (1996) talks of the role of support groups for black students but both students in the study stated that they would not go to such a group even if it existed. Further work needs to be done to understand why black students may not want groups specifically to support black students.

Secondly, there is no way of knowing the real attitudes of some of the students who have successfully got through the admission procedures. It has suggested that candidates should be screened more closely at interviews, but Jones's (1998) work indicates that some students are conscious of their ability to play sophisticated games and are skilled at presenting the politically correct self when necessary. The argument for better establishment awareness of discriminatory attitudes of students and their consequences is thus strengthened.

Thirdly, this is no reason to feel complacent regarding the equal opportunities policy of the institution or that further training of staff and students is no longer necessary. Bird (1996) comments on the ill-founded notion that the liberal academy is not a site of discrimination, echoing Siraj-Blatchford's (1993) words of three years earlier referred to at the beginning of this chapter.

Finally, the complexity of life-history is now clear, as well as its importance of providing vulnerable students with the opportunity to explore narratives of the self (Bird, 1996). Exposing such pain will be able to help empower those students who feel powerless. The moral burden on the researcher, however, is a heavy and complex one. In the words of Bird (1996, p6):

> There is a need for a critical ethnography which is aware of the positioning of researchers and those they study, and which is therefore, reflexive.

Overall, there is a very clear case for institutional policies that can effectively deal with the experiences of students, however small the number, in a framework which cuts across departments and areas of student experiences.

Bibliography

Bird, J. (1996), *Black Students and Higher Education, Rhetorics and Realities*, Open University Press, Buckingham, UK.

Jones, R. (1997), *Deafening Silence: Telling Stories of Beginnng Teachers' Understanding of Ethnicity*, unpublished PhD Thesis, Manchester Metropolitan University, UK.

Jones, R. (1999), *Teaching Racism - or Tackling it?: Multicultural Stories from Beginning White Teachers*, Trentham Books, Stoke-on-Trent, UK.

Maguire, M., Jones, C. and Watson, B. et al. (1996), *Nothing to Lose and Something to Tell, Four Black Trainee Teachers' Stories of Their In-School Experiences*, Paper for the National Initiatives and Equality Issues Inaugural Conference, University of Hertfordshire, UK.

Siraj-Blatchford, I. (1993), Social Justice and Teacher Education in the UK, in Verma, G. (ed.), *Inequality and Teacher Education*, Falmer Press, London.

7 Male Students on Primary Initial Teacher Education Courses

MARY THORNTON

Abstract

For a few decades in the twentieth century the focus in the context of gender issues was specifically on how girls and women were adversely affected in areas such as education and employment. As would be appropriate in a true consideration of aspects of gender, attention has turned to bringing boys and men into the framework. This chapter highlights one specific context.

In England and Wales 20 per cent of primary teachers and approximately 10 per cent of primary BEd students are male. Research suggests that in England, around 80 per cent of primary teachers are female but around 50 per cent of head teachers are male. While males may have very successful primary school teaching careers they are much more likely to fail or withdraw from their initial training course. There is concern about this gender imbalance. This chapter discusses ongoing research which is focused on initial teacher education course entrance and experience that explores these gender patterns in the background of structured gender inequalities in the British educational labour market. By analysing perceptions of male students, issues regarding the strength of stereotyping emerge which may provide real challenges for educators and policy makers. This chapter also demonstrates the incompleteness of an equation which aims to solve a problem simply by targeting an increase in number.

Introduction

Current research suggests that, in England, around 80 per cent of primary teachers are female but around 50 per cent of head teachers are male (Alexander, 1991). Males therefore appear to have disproportionate control over decision making in primary schools. In contrast in the training phase of (Initial Teacher Education) (ITE), around 10 per cent of students are male. Evidence here suggests that while males may have very successful primary school teaching careers they are much more likely to fail or withdraw from their initial training course. This chapter will discuss research in progress that explores gender patterns in

- recruitment to primary teacher education;
- male experiences of teacher education;
- success and failure rates whilst in training;
- first appointments;
- career paths.

In England and Wales 20 per cent of primary teachers and approximately 10 per cent of primary BEd students are male. As we enter the new millennium concern is being expressed about this gender imbalance, by the National Association of Head Teachers (NAHT, 1995), and the Teacher Training Agency (TTA, 1996), whose Chief Executive at that time, Anthea Millett (1995), stated that this concern related to '... their position as role models...'. In response to such concerns the TTA is offering increased student allocations to teacher training institutions that demonstrate 'distinctiveness' by recruiting a minimum of twenty percent male students to their primary BEd and PGCE courses.

That men are frequently successful in making a career out of primary teaching is self-evident. For example, 50 per cent of primary head teachers in England and Wales are male despite males constituting just under 20 per cent of this teaching force. Research undertaken by Edwards and Lyons (1996) found that males are much more likely to be heads of junior schools, and of the biggest primary schools, where pay is higher, and that this established pattern gets stronger and stronger the further one moves away from the capital, London.

Past quantitative research has revealed these structural inequalities (Thornton, 1997). Building on that, this chapter explores perceptions of male students to recruitment to, and experiences of, primary ITE through qualitative questionnaires and interviews. In doing so it seeks to make problematic the view that more men, pure quantity, would automatically be a good thing for primary education. Structured gender inequalities in the British educational labour market form the background context to this ongoing research which is focused on ITE entrance and course experience, initial teaching appointments, areas of responsibility and promotion prospects. Gender inequalities clearly impact upon the nature of the role models available to children in our primary schools (which have predominantly female staff but men disproportionately occupying positions of power), and are raised as issues by males participating in this research. However, questions concerning equity of treatment between men and women regarding their teaching careers and the importance or not of appropriate role models for primary children, are not overtly addressed in this chapter; the focus here is on the perceptions and experiences of male primary ITE students operating (successfully or not) as a minority group within the female dominated professional field of primary teacher education.

Quantitative Background

Gender differences within education are not new. Despite the narrowing of gaps in recent years, males in England and Wales are still more likely than females to study to advanced levels maths, technology and science-based subjects, and females are more likely to do the same in the humanities and arts-based subjects. These differences can be seen not only in the gender distribution of secondary and higher education subject-based teachers but also between male and female subject co-ordinators in primary schools (Thornton, 1996).

John Patten, former British Secretary of State for Education, proposed a 'mums army' of non-graduate and differentially trained nursery and Key Stage 1 (5 to 7 years) teachers. He made explicit and overt the usually implicit low status of primary teachers. His 'mums army' proposal clearly illustrated, and made public, teacher stratification within the educational division of labour, although he did not invent it. This stratification of teachers has a long history covering the latter half of this century and permeating the consciousness of many parents and the general public as well as politicians. Patten's 'mums army' proposal publicly confirmed primary teachers' lower status by identifying lower (than degree level) qualifications as acceptable for teacher's of young children. It also explicitly confirmed higher status of teachers of older children, an age-phase where UK male primary teachers are much more likely to be found. The primary teacher, male or female, occupies a different and more lowly power/status position to that of the secondary school teacher of GCSE and A Level subjects or the higher education lecturer, but the primary teacher is also much more likely to be female. For teachers in England, higher status (and subsequent authority and power) goes with the teaching of older pupils, having an overt subject identity (especially if that subject identity is maths or science), and maleness (Thornton, 1996). Similar patterns and issues of gender-related power/status have emerged from other studies with a different focal point e.g. Loizou and Rossiter's (1987) study of the role of maths post-holders, and Alexander's (1991) study of the role of 'primary needs' co-ordinators in Leeds. Table 7.1 summarises the initial findings of this earlier part of the research in relation to gender inequality in teaching positions.

Table 7.1 Gender inequality in teaching positions

Position	% Male (N.250)	% Female (N. 16221)
Headteachers	135	7
Deputies	17	9
Allowance-Holders	13	23
Non-Allowance Holders	32	53
Floating	3	8
Total	100	100

It should be noted that the majority of female teachers (61 per cent) are on main professional grade (MPG), holding no additional allowances or management positions, and that the majority of male teachers (65 per cent) are on salaries above MPG, as allowance holders or as part of the senior management team. Over a third of the males in the sample have achieved headship of a primary school while only 7 per cent of the female teachers have done so. It is suggested by the chi-squared tests that these differences are statistically significant (0.0000). There may be relatively few male teachers in this sample (N=250, 13 per cent) but once qualified and in post they appear to have excellent career prospects.

At a simplistic and somewhat superficial level, female teachers may enhance their career prospects by specialising in higher status subjects such as maths, science and information technology (IT), and the teaching of older children (Key Stage 2: 8 to 11 years, but 10 and 11 year olds especially). However, Alexander's (1991) work suggests that if women are in competition with men for these posts they are less likely to get them and if they do get them then they are less likely to get a salary increase as a result.

Quantitative data, such as that outlined above, enables the identification of patterns of gender inequality within the education system. It also makes possible an effective challenging of simplistic suggestions that increased recruitment of males into primary teaching will resolve the gender imbalance of role models experienced by children. The situation is clearly more complex than that.

Given the career profiles indicated above one might be tempted to think that male entrants into UK primary teacher training are few but of particularly high quality. Experiential and formal knowledge of undergraduate and post graduate ITE courses in several institutions, together with a tentative analysis of longitudinal cohort data, suggests otherwise (Table 7.2). Many males appear to fail, or withdraw from, their training courses. Males are disproportionately represented in the lower classes of the degree classification system (third class and unclassified degrees). Male recruitment may be low and, others have argued, in need of expansion, but an improved completion rate would go some way towards addressing primary teacher gender imbalance if that were demonstrated to be educationally worthwhile.

That male ITE students fail, in disproportionate numbers, to complete their training courses satisfactorily, is clearly indicated in the cohort analysis of BEd students at a new university in an English shire county (Table 7.2). The sample cited here relates to one course in one university and it could be argued to be untypical. However, formal and informal experience of a range of ITE institutions and their courses, including PGCE, would seem to confirm the general pattern of males being less successful than females.

Non-completion for male students through withdrawal, course change or failure ranged from 27 per cent to 50 per cent and for females from 6 per cent to 18 per cent; clearly a significant gender difference. If final year failure, the award of an unclassified degree and/or third class degrees were to be taken into account then male students on this sample can be seen to be effectively unsuccessful at a rate between 55.5 per cent and 66 per cent. Taking the example of the 1992-1996 BEd cohort, there was a total of nine males in Year 1. Out of the six who completed the final year, one failed, bringing the loss in real terms to 44 per cent. Of the remaining five, one got an unclassified, and another one a third class, degree. Therefore, only three male students were successful in gaining a good honours degree, 33 per cent of the original nine.

Table 7.2 Gender analysis of ITE cohorts

ITE Students	Males	Females	Fem loss % (no)	Male loss % (no)
1992-1996 BEd Cohort				
Year 1 total 131	9	122		
Year 4 total 119	6	113	7.4% (9)	33% (3)
1991-1995 BEd Cohort				
Year 1 total 150	18	132		
Year 4 total 119	9	110	17% (22)	50% (9)
1990-1994 BEd Cohort				
Year 1 total 118	8	110		
Year 4 total 99	5	94	14.5% (16)	37% (3)
1994-1995 PGCE				
Total 69	13	56	18% (10)	31% (4)
1993-4 PGCE				
Total 92	11	18	6% (5)	27% (3)

The withdrawal/failure rates on PGCE primary courses appear lower, perhaps because mature students tend to achieve better results in higher education than students straight from school (Nye, 1996) but there remain substantial differences between male and female ITE students. There is a variety of possible explanations for this which warrant further exploration. Smedley and Pepperell (1996) have studied male student perceptions of a BA with a QTS (Qualified Teacher Status) course but comparisons between undergraduate and post graduate male ITE student experiences have yet to be fully researched. Some male students may feel intimidated by a predominantly female peer group but this would not explain differences between undergraduate and post graduate withdrawal/failure rates. Females clearly dominate both types of primary ITE routes. It is, however, possible that post graduate ITE students, being older and more mature, have a firmer commitment to their chosen career in primary teaching and have already had their academic ability thoroughly tested through their undergraduate studies. It is the perceptions of male BEd students, both mature and standard age entry, that need to be analysed. However, rather than male recruitment 'distinctiveness', the TTA might wish to consider retention and success rates as an important starting point in understanding and then perhaps redressing the gender imbalance in primary teaching in England in Wales.

Male BEd Student Perceptions

The qualitative sample covered male BEd students at the end of their first year and those completing their fourth year in 1997. All were sent open ended questionnaires with an invitation to 'talk further' through a follow-up interview. The response rate was disappointing but the quality of the responses received was high. However, given the number of responses from an initially small sample, caution must be exercised in drawing any conclusions from the views expressed. It was valuable to receive the thoughts and comments of both successful male students and those experiencing some difficulties. Normally one would be required to view the comments of continuing students with caution, as they may be less likely to be critical (despite promises of confidentiality) of their course and experiences. However, their views were largely in accord with the respondents from year four, who were leaving, with jobs, and had nothing to fear from free expression.

Year 1 had thirteen male, out of a total of one hundred and sixteen students. Questionnaires were returned by three of the eight males who passed, and two of the five who were deferred/referred. One from each category was interviewed. Year 4 had seven male out of a total on one hundred and twenty six students. All seven passed and three both returned the questionnaires and were interviewed.

Both the questionnaires and interviews were open-ended, asking for views, experiences, ideas and suggestions about male students and ITE. All but two wrote long detailed responses to the questions and all interviewees gave their time freely to expound on their written responses. Key issues emerging from the interviews and questionnaires are outlined below. These male students focused their ideas primarily around 'maturity', 'careers', 'male problems' and perceived potential solutions.

Maturity

As in many English ITE courses there was a large number of mature students, male and female, on this BEd (between 30 and 40 per cent in any one year). More than half the respondents were mature males, defined as aged over twenty one at the start of their course. These students found family responsibilities and pressures to be more problematic than the fact of being male students. They talked about late timetabling affecting child-minding arrangements and the need to spend time with their families while at the same time working hard towards their degrees. On the positive side they felt that their maturity enabled them to get on well with the female majority on their course; they were more outgoing and confident than younger males might be; they were clear about the reasons for their studies as an overt career choice and they were committed to primary teaching as a career. They claimed, on the whole, to be well organised e.g. getting assignments completed in good time, and to be working hard. They recognised that their problems, as derived from being mature students, were also experienced by mature female students. One example was that of a student seeking a first appointment (Dick, BEd 4):

> I felt I was discriminated against in actually getting a job ... it would be interesting to see how the mature female students felt but I definitely felt that what a lot of heads wanted was a 22 year old that they could mould. I came out of here with very definite opinions and came across, as the careers lady said, you come across as very committed and that is intimidating, frightening to heads, and I can understand that. So actually as a mature student, I've got my job now so it's easy to reflect on it, but at the same time it was actually quite anxious, because I didn't have the option of thinking I'll take a year out. The anxiety was quite high, so it's actually been quite difficult to start and I definitely felt that heads were looking for, well, malleable males the person they are employing seem soft but... I would hesitate to say that it was a male thing, but I would say it was a mature thing.

Careers

Males appeared to choose primary teaching for idealistic reasons as well as pragmatic ones. These students variously said they had always wanted to teach; it was enjoyable, challenging, rewarding; they were influenced by good experiences of primary teachers during their own schooling; that a vocation was more important than money; that primary education was the building block of education, socially vital, and that they wanted and were committed to contributing to it. Dick (BEd 4) stated that it 'deserves to have the highest calibre and most dedicated professionals within it' He was not sure if he fitted that role, 'but I'd like to aspire to it'.

Most of these students also felt that primary children would benefit from male presence in their classrooms. Some said this was due to the rise of single parent families and the lack, for many young children, of a male role model in their lives. Charles (BEd 1) believed that 'children need male role models at this impressionable age, especially where there are lone parents'.

This emphasis on commitment and worthwhileness was emphasised by all but one student, but this also stood alongside a general commitment to making a career out of primary teaching. These male students did not romanticise their work with young children in the way that some primary teachers might. It was a valuable and worthwhile job but one which they also saw as leading to fairly rapid promotion and the possibility of at least adequate monetary reward (eventually). In the opinion of Tom (BEd 4):

> I've been cheered, as a male, by the fact that my career prospects appear that much better. And in that way it's made me think, well yes, I can come into teaching on a low salary and then three years on look for a deputy headship, maybe another four years look for a headship, and be quick about it because in that way I can move up the scale.... Is that because we are male or because we are more career minded, in the sense that we want to get ahead of the pack for those reasons, because we have a family to support?

Carl's (BEd 4) opinion was that 'Sexist though it may be, there are excellent career prospects for male primary school teachers'. A career in teaching was seen to be particularly attractive as a second income, which might explain why some mature males, with wives or partners in secure jobs, consider it as a second career, after redundancy taking the example of Dick (BEd 4):

> For me (as a mature student) it was a definite decision, not a whim, to go to university...it's a leap of faith by your partner as well. You are necessarily committed... the aim for me was to get a job, to retrain, and to do a job I want to do rather than just get a degree and hope I can go into middle management somewhere.

These male students tended to have very clear intentions of making progress in their primary teaching careers and to get promotion. Most of them had plans to move quickly through the pay scales and into management although they also recognised that teaching was not a career to be primarily chosen to become rich. The intention on the part of some male students to make rapid progress in their careers is matched by an awareness that their rarity value, as males, makes them a desirable commodity, which they can use to further their careers. Tom (BEd 4) showed concern that:

> It's one of those things. Because there's a shortage of males... schools are more likely to push you ahead... in order to keep those males. But if you boost the amount of men in the profession then career prospects drop.

Dick (BEd 4) had the experience of

> another school chasing me already so I'm going to play two heads against each other and I'm going to see if I can't get some financial benefit.

However, if male recruitment to primary teaching were to rapidly increase, then career advantages based on short supply/rarity value could disappear.

These students did see some problems for themselves and other males (but usually other males) in primary ITE. The problems identified related to context and perceived male characteristics rather than the content of ITE courses, with which all seemed to express varying degrees of satisfaction. None sought to change course content at all as a means of reducing male student drop out/failure rates. What they did suggest to be influencing factors were friendships/support networks, social perceptions, and 'standing out'.

Friendship and support networks   Although no respondent said that they personally lacked friends or support most cited this as crucial to success and potentially difficult to achieve for male students due to their small number and what they perceived to be a male propensity to not share their problems or difficulties with others. Alex (BEd 1):

> found it good to have a friend of mine, another male, in the same school (Teaching Experience- TE) ... it was fairly strange being in a female dominated profession ... (It was) valuable to compare experiences, exchange ideas and enjoy the TE.

Dick (BEd 4) had some views about gender differences:

> I've not really felt any kind of discrimination within the course, if you like, because the occasion hasn't arisen, because I've just

nipped it in the bud myself. Perhaps male pride might come in to it; admission of a problem ... Men tend to be more solo don't they. Women will ... in general ... be more gregarious as a group, a network, for example, he blew his year 4 TE, referred, because he bottled all bottled all his stress, despite the fact that Tom and I, for example, his little group, could see he was under stress and were trying to reassure him. He never actually sought, or requested, or opened up in anyway, help from us. You can try to give advice but if the man's not listening he's not going to take it, and there's nothing you can do. And basically, because of the stress he felt he was under and couldn't express...even to his friends, he blew it, week 2 of TE. None of us knew about it. He never phoned any of us. So, I'm wondering if X isn't actually more typical of males.

Charles (BEd 1) felt that men traditionally are reputed to be less able to share their feelings. Maybe this contributes to the male wastage rate. Other students also thought that males were less inclined to share their feelings and experiences of the course than females. There may also be an element of males wanting to 'save face'. Male culture, according to these male students, appears to say that they must succeed (at least over women). To admit failure might damage their reputation and undermine their gender association with the 'successful male' image. Mature male students perceived this to be more of a problem for standard age entry male students than it was for them personally, but that in itself may be indicative of male potential to avoid being perceived as in need of help or support. Clearly everyone needs someone to share disappointments with. Mature males and married males may find it easier to share with females than do the younger male students. The mature male respondents appeared (and claimed) to be confident and experienced enough not to feel threatened by a predominantly female environment. The question then would be how to enable younger male students to make this transition and access the support, both male and female, that is available to them from fellow students. As Charles (BEd 1) notes, the sheer number of females, in teaching practice schools and on the course, makes primary teaching appear to be a natural job for women whilst at the same time leading to feelings of insecurity amongst male students.

Social perceptions The view amongst these students that primary teaching is thought of as a good second income, but not really sufficient as the income for the main or sole bread winner has already been noted. While these men saw themselves largely on a fast track to a good career and rapid promotion they also suggested that primary teaching does not attract males because it is seen as low paid, with low status attached to it. Males, they perceived, were attracted to high status, highly paid jobs. If one adds to this the view that boys may seek to follow in their fathers' footsteps one can perhaps see why so few males choose primary teaching as a career, especially at age eighteen. For females primary teaching may, socially, be viewed as an extension of their mothering role (Alex BEd 1), but when males opt for primary teaching it is perceived as odd. They are even considered potential child molesters (Alistair BEd Yr). As Tom (BEd 4) noted:

> I was chatting to my grandmother, about coming here (to talk to researcher) and she said was that because men shouldn't be in primary classrooms. I thought thanks!... I've also found it's a low self-esteem sort of job in some ways for men...from their point of view (and) how others view them...it's not a thing that a man should be doing.

Whatever the exhortations of the TTA or others, primary teaching in England (and probably in many other countries) is still not seen as 'masculine' work, and the evidence available clearly demonstrates that it is female work. Male students and teachers are greeted with excitement, awe or fear, by parents, pupils, other teachers, governors and head teachers, precisely because they are rare and their presence does not conform to the gender stereotypes of primary teaching.

Standing out While the course content was found by these male students to be not discriminatory, to be gender neutral, enjoyable and often challenging, there was one aspect of the context in which their ITE had taken place that they felt could be addressed. That was 'standing out'. They were aware that as a small minority of students on the course males stood out, but they did not want or like that to be exacerbated by the way in which they were treated by tutors. Tom (BEd 4) expressed his views as follows:

> The most important thing that you can do is not point out that there are men in the class. I think that is really bad. The first example was in UTL (professional course on teaching and learning) where we got up and we had to write our name on the board to say who we were. So you wrote your name on the board and everybody said, 'Oh we know who you are. We're not going to get your name wrong because you're a man', you know, the only man in the group. So immediately I'm thinking, Oh God, I'm the only man in

the group ... I found it difficult in my first year, in UTL groups, being the only male, in halls, being the only male education student, and that's something that needs to be looked at.

To highlight the presence of lone/small numbers of male students was thought to simply reinforce the strangeness of being males amongst females. It made them stand out in situations where the male students wished to be treated 'the same' as female students.

Perceived solutions These students have little to offer the TTA or ITE tutors in terms of how to improve courses in order to enhance male recruitment and success rates because they do not perceive the courses to be the cause (or solution) to the problem. Dick (BEd 4) could not 'see what it is on the course. I can't see what it is that would turn somebody off other than it not being the right decision'. Similarly Tim (BEd 4) found it very difficult to answer the question about what could be changed because 'I honestly think that things that everybody has moaned about has been the same whether they are male or female'.

These students would variously advise male recruits to work hard and not get behind; to make friends and talk to them when they have problems, and to not to be afraid of asking for help, from friends or tutors. Before deciding on a career in primary teaching they suggested pre-experience to be essential, to ensure that it was really what the student wanted to do, and to avoid misunderstandings about what primary teaching involves. Beyond this their advice addressed issues that are not within the control of ITE institutions. Males, they said, must be encouraged to view primary teaching as a suitable career. Its image (and reality) as a stereotypical, low status female occupation must be challenged and changed. Teachers in general were undervalued, but primary teachers especially. Males, especially good quality candidates, would not choose it as a career while it was associated with low pay and low status. In Dick's (BEd 4) opinion:

> to raise standards so the teaching may be far more competitive, like the other professions, 3 A's (Grade A at A Level) should be needed. But then you have got to have a salary, at the end of the day, to reflect that.

Tom (BEd 4) echoed that:

> I think (status) is the real key issue... especially something like the BEd degree. I meet lots of my friends who've gone off and got their BA (Bachelor of Arts)... and they almost view their degree as

superior to mine... I think it's important that the status of the degree is heightened, publicly, because I think the more that people continue to chide and knock at it because we're an easy target... the less respected we get and it's likely ...men, who like respect, who won't want to be viewed poorly, stay away...

Only one respondent argued for positive discrimination in favour of men. Others felt it was more important to have the best candidates, whatever their gender.

Chickens and Eggs

There is a strong sense of 'chickens and eggs' in seeking solutions to problems identified by these male students on primary ITE courses and in recruiting them to such courses. The main chicken and egg problem concerns numbers. Males are in short supply, between 10 per cent and 15 per cent of many primary BEd cohorts, and around 20 per cent of primary teachers in post. The shortage of numbers means that there are fewer role models for males to emulate, especially in viewing primary teaching as a suitable male career. Male justification for choosing primary teaching is made difficult because of its image as a stereotypically female profession. Because it is female dominated, and associated with young children it attracts lower pay and status than some male dominated occupations. There are fewer male students with whom other males can identify and build support networks or friendship groups with. However, if there were more men in primary teaching then:

- there would be more role models to emulate;
- it might be seen as a more suitable male career;
- it would not be viewed as a stereotypically female profession;
- justifications for males choosing it as a career would be made easier;
- it might attract higher pay and status;
- male student support networks and friendship groups would be stronger.

Basically these arguments are circular. There are too few males in primary teaching because there too few males in primary teaching. To get more males into primary teaching more males have to go into primary teaching. Exhortations alone, or justifications put forward on the basis of children's argued educational need for more male role models, will not be enough to remedy the problems perceived by these male students. Public and personal attitudes would need to be changed, alongside external input to raise the pay and status of primary teachers. The down side for male primary teachers of such an unlikely turn of events would be that their individual value might drop, as they would cease to be a rare commodity, thereby diminishing their apparent current advantages in the career/promotion stakes.

Conclusion

Gender inequality in recruitment is likely to remain a feature of primary ITE well into the millennium unless direct, external and long term action is taken. Male experience of ITE can be addressed by seeking to support male students more and in attempting to get them to be more open about any difficulties they may experience. However, from these students' viewpoints, there is nothing inherent in their ITE courses that they believe could be changed in order to enhance male recruitment or success rates. Their perceptions of male failure relate more to their understanding of stereotypical male characteristics. These are points which ITE can seek to address but is unlikely to be able remedy independently of their wider social causes.

Gender was not perceived as a key issue in first appointments to primary teaching posts. Maturity was felt by some to hinder their range of opportunities. However, once in post, these males students had clearly mapped out, expected and would seek, rapid promotion to the managerial layers of primary teaching. Their aspirations were high and that, at least in part, played a key role in their choice of career. Quantitative evidence suggests that many of the male ITE students will achieve their desired rapid promotion into management positions.

The stereotypical male gender characteristics identified by these male students should be questioned and challenged, wherever they impact upon primary ITE and primary teaching as a career. Primary ITE should be, but is not, as open and accessible in terms of success rates for male students as it is for female students. Conversely, employment and promotion once qualified should be determined by teaching ability, not gender rarity.

Bibliography

Alexander, R. (1991), *Primary Education in Leeds: Twelfth and final report from the Primary Needs Independent Evaluation Project*, University of Leeds, UK.

Edwards, S. and Lyons, G. (1996), 'It's Grim Up North for Female High Flyers', *TES School Management Guide*, 10 May, p.2.

Loizou, C. D. and Rossiter, D. (1987), *The Role of the Mathematics Post-Holder in Primary School*, University of Birmingham, UK.

Millett, A. (1995), *Times Education Supplement*, September 8, p.22.

National Association of Head Teachers (1995), *Early Years Education: The Entitlement to Quality*, NAHT, London.

Nye, M. (1996), 'How to Read the Signposts, Synthesis Trends', *Times Higher Education Supplement*, 27 September, pp.iv-v.

Smedley, S. and Pepperell, S. (1996), *Male Student Primary Teachers*, Paper presented at University of London Institute of Education, September.

Teacher Training Agency, (1996), *Invitation to Bid for Initial Teacher Training Allocations for 1997/8, 1998/9 and 1999/2000*, TTA, London.

Thornton, M. (1996), 'Subject Specialism, Gender and Status: The Example of Primary School Mathematics', in *Education 3 to 13*, vol. 2, no. 3, pp. 52-54.

Thornton, M. (1997), 'Men into Primary Teaching: Dilemmas of Entry, Survival and Career Progression', pp.136-146 in Shah, S. (ed), *National Initiatives and Equality Issues*, Centre for Equality Issues in Education, University of Hertfordshire, UK.

8 A New Millennium for Disabled Students in Higher Education?

LEA MYERS AND VIV PARKER

Abstract

Disabled students have been 'invisible' in higher education (HE) for many years. They have difficulty getting access to university and in receiving equal treatment once in. This chapter outlines some recent changes and research in Britain and demonstrates how these have led to developments in awareness of the barriers and keys to equality of access to learning. The authors also consider pedagogical issues such as the ways in which different teaching and learning styles facilitate or hamper learners.

As a result of the advances made in recent years those institutions which have done most to promote access have become more aware of the barriers and keys to equality of access to learning. Considerations of physical access to the learning environment and identification of central support services, together with staff awareness of disability issues, provide a good foundation upon which to radically challenge much that is taken for granted in higher education.

If disabled students are to be fully included in higher education then we have to ensure that they have access to the full higher education experience including extra-curricular activities. To accommodate disability issues in HE there will need to be more emphasis on the quality of teaching and learning, so that staff are encouraged to consider whether their teaching methods match the learning styles of diverse groups of students and how they can match this diversity.

The new millennium should begin with us asking the right questions about the barriers to full inclusion, listening to the voices of disabled students and their representative organisations, and making honest efforts to reduce and remove the barriers.

Introduction

In so many ways, the impediments to access which face disabled students stand proxy for the impediments faced by all under-represented groups (Robertson and Hillman, 1997).

The year 2000 it a good time to take stock of where we are now in terms of access to HE in the United Kingdom and to consider, in the light of recent developments, whether the new century will herald a different and better millennium for the education for all presently under-represented groups in the sector, including disabled students.

Disabled students have been 'invisible' in HE for many years. They have difficulty getting access to university and in receiving equal treatment once in. This chapter focuses on recent research in the HE sector undertaken, at the University of East London, in collaboration with SKILL - the National Bureau for Students with Disabilities, and the working experience of the staff. Will the next decade see the implementation of new practices in the sector which will remove those barriers to learning which presently disable many students and potential students?

Where are we Now?

In addressing the question of where we are now it is necessary to focus on three recent developments. Firstly, the National Committee of Inquiry into Higher Education under Sir Ron Dearing (1997) which '...set(s) out a vision for the future development of higher education in a learning society...' (Blunkett, 1997, p.1) and whose recommendations are beginning to have a profound influence on every aspect of HE. Secondly, there will be an analysis of changes to the sector as a result of the implementation of the Disability Discrimination Act (1995) and thirdly, the results of HEFCE (Higher Education Funding Council (England)) funding initiatives to widen participation and improve quality will be examined.

Dearing on Provision for Disabled Students

Dearing noted the consensus that data on participation of disabled students is unreliable. The Higher Education Statistics Agency (HESA) compile and publish figures on participation, and whilst these data are probably the most reliable and extensive thus far (HEFCE, 1996), it is believed by many university co-ordinators for students with disabilities that they are not accurate. Universities themselves do not know how many students they have with impairments. Some universities collect their own data, but the figures are determined by the ways in which they define disability. For example Robertson and Hillman (1997) in their report to the National Committee of Inquiry, pointed to epilepsy which is a disability in one institution but not in another one, 'depending on whether an institution believed it required intervention or not'. Applicants to university are invited by UCAS (Universities Central Admissions Service) to tick a box to indicate that they have a disability. Some who tick the box may not need any additional support (O'Hanlon and Manning, 1994), whilst some '...appear to misunderstand the question, interpreting a declaration of a special need' as a request for childcare, financial support, or a preference for a vegetarian diet' (Robertson and Hillman, 1997). Other applicants, however, may not tick the box because they are concerned that doing so may prejudice their chances of being offered a place, or because they do not want any favours and want to achieve on their own merit. In addition, UCAS is not a comprehensive service since it does not cover all classes of student e.g. applicants for part-time study and postgraduate study do not apply through UCAS. Nevertheless, despite the unreliability of the data there is general agreement that disabled students are under-represented in the sector. This is in contrast to the school and further education (FE) sectors which, over the past decade, have developed their understanding of disability and have had increasing numbers of disabled students successfully completing their studies. Those students are now demanding access to higher education and finding that the sector is less well advanced in understanding than school and FE. The difficulties students may face when attempting to make the transition from further to higher education are illustrated with reference to recent applicants to the authors' own institution.

Over a period of a few months recently, the University of East London (UEL) had requests from four deaf applicants all asking if interpreter support is provided by the University for open-day events. Deaf students studying full-time in Higher Education may draw on a maximum of £10,000 per year from the disabled student allowance (DSA) to pay for note-takers and interpreters, but no funding is given to support applicants in exploring what courses and opportunities are available to them before they make a decision about their final application. Applicants in these four cases were denied an opportunity to benefit from the open days.

Information from the tutors at the FE colleges from which the enquiries came indicated that they found the lack of interpreter support for these events to be widespread across the HE sector.

Whilst lack of support for applicants is common, Dearing found that there were some institutions which have done much to develop their practices and had a commitment to funding developments in the area. These institutions attracted students because they were prepared to offer quality provision and bear the cost, whilst some other institutions had made no effort at all to attract disabled students. Dearing commented, too, on the financial arrangements for supporting disabled students, which discriminated against part-time study and which are means tested. So, for example, disabled students who study part-time, or those whose parents were earning above the limit for qualification for a maintenance grant, were not eligible for the DSA. In these cases students were required to fund both their studies and their additional support needs. These latter arrangements have changed in the academic year 1998/1999. Dearing summarised that:

- HE does not have a well focused understanding of disability;
- there is unevenness of practice in how institutions manage the cost burdens of disabled students;
- disability awareness is poorly developed in most institutions of HE among academic staff, administrators and senior management;
- the means tested character of the DSA places an unfair burden on parents.

Amongst recommendations to generate a culture and environment where disability is not regarded as a problem (Robertson and Hillman, 1997) was the suggestion that universities and colleges should be included within the terms of the Disability Discrimination Act (1995) (DDA).

Disability Discrimination Act, 1995

Currently higher education institutions (HEIs) are excluded from the main clauses of the Act which brought in new laws and measures aimed at ending the discrimination which many disabled people face (Disability on the Agenda, 1995). The Act ensures recognition of the needs of disabled people who want to study and 'the provision of better information for parents, pupils and students'. It places a statutory duty on university funding councils to have regard to the needs of disabled persons and requires the governing bodies of institutions of higher education funded by them to publish disability statements outlining their provision. However, funding councils were already taking measures to increase participation for students with disabilities prior to the passing of the Act.

HEFCE Projects to Improve Access 1993-1995

In recognition of the need to improve access to HE for students with disabilities HEFCE offered £3 million in 1993/1994 for projects of one year duration designed to increase participation of students with disabilities. This was followed with a further, similar, tranche in the following year. All projects had to be action/outcome directed, so solely research-directed activities were not supported. The total number of projects funded over the two years was eighty-six, and these were located across fifty nine institutions (twenty seven institutions were funded across both years). Between one half and one third of the total number of institutions of higher education in England were directly involved in some way. Dissemination events and materials have ensured that many of the institutions not funded for projects have been given the opportunity to benefit from them. The main achievements of the projects were:

- raising the profile of support for disability within institutions, and increasing awareness among staff, especially central services staff, of the needs of students with disabilities;
- improving access to the curriculum for particular groups of students with disabilities by co-ordinating internal support services and making it easier for students to find support;
- increasing and sharing information, resources and advice for students with disabilities and staff across the whole sector;
- developing new electronic sources of advice as projects set newsgroups and bulletin boards on the Internet and their own World Wide Web pages.

Most of the funded institutions recorded great increase in the numbers of students with disabilities applying, entering and making their needs known.

HEFCE Projects to Improve Access 1996-1997

HEFCE has followed up these initiatives by offering a further £4.92 million for projects of three years' duration concerned with improving the quality of provision, and with an emphasis on collaboration. UEL has successfully bid at each of the three phases of funding for HEFCE. Overall, thirty one development plans have been successful in bidding, covering:

- learning support or curriculum access;
- staff development or dissemination;
- establishing a resource or assessment centre;
- transition into/out of HE;
- dyslexia, sensory impairment, mental health and/or physical disability;
- collaboration.

An examination of the latest criteria for funding projects, as well as the project outlines themselves, suggests a developing awareness of a social model of disability. The emphasis has shifted from a focus on getting students into HE, to creating effective learning environments by collaboration within and across institutions. Nevertheless, because these funding initiatives were concerned to build upon existing good practice there remained a considerable number of institutions which had not benefited from the funding and had not participated in the dissemination events. The HEFCE report on the 1993/1994 and 1994/1995 special initiatives referred to the problem that 'many non-participating institutions do not have a named member of staff with whom participating institutions can share their expertise' (HEFCE, 1996). Thus those institutions which bid for, and won, funds for special projects were facilitated in disseminating best practice between themselves, but in the institutions with little or no awareness and provision for students with disabilities (a little under one half of the institutions funded in the sector) there was limited or no progress. It was within this context that the University of East London and SKILL worked together to carry out research about disability statements and aimed to identify:

- the processes and personnel likely to be involved in generating the disability statements;

- any anticipated positive and/or negative effects on the information and services made available to students by the requirement to produce the statement.

Disability Statements

The date for publication of Disability Statements in England was 10th January, 1997. The requirement to publish a statement seemed initially to be a very modest requirement and unlikely to have any significant impact on improving access to HE for applicants with disabilities. The main purpose of the statements is that they should describe the facilities for education and research that an HEI offers people with disabilities, with a secondary purpose of informing the Funding Council of such provision and to 'highlight good practice which the Council may draw upon in the future' (HEFCE, 1996). Since the legislation concerns only the supply of information it was feared by many practitioners and observers that the level and quality of provision in the sector would remain largely untouched. However, research conducted by the authors indicates that even such a modest requirement has had a small but significant effect upon the sector. Although there was no requirement for HEIs to offer any provision which might support disabled students, it seems that few institutions were prepared to issue a statement indicating that they had no such provision. Accordingly, the requirement to publish a statement detailing provision seems to have been a first step in drawing matters of disability access to the attention of senior managers of those institutions which, hitherto, may have never considered the matter.

The production of a statement is a process which necessitates institutional audits of policy and provision, and this has served to raise the profile and increase awareness of disability issues within institutions. Staff have been identified to collate information, and in some cases these individuals have also been named as the university's disability co-ordinator. Sector wide improvements in the information available will enable applicants to make an informed choice about where to study, and will support students on course by naming a person to contact for help and advice, and clearly indicating to them what they can expect as a minimum provision.

Summary of the Current Situation

The last decade has seen a number of developments in terms of facilitating access to higher education for students with disabilities. As a result of the requirement under the DDA (1995) for universities to publish disability statements, all HEIs now have a named person who students, staff and outside agencies can contact for information and advice. Applicants can now make better informed choices about where to study based on details about courses, as well as the level of support that each institution offers for their particular learning need. The profile of disability within the higher education sector has been raised, as has senior management's awareness of disability issues.

As a result of the first two years of HEFCE funding initiatives a sizeable number of institutions have been involved in projects aimed at promoting access to information, the curriculum and learning support for students with disabilities. These projects have developed centres of excellence, and disseminated best practice, thus raising the profile of disability across the sector. They have increased the awareness of staff within participating institutions, resulting in improved access to the curriculum for particular groups of students through the co-ordination of internal support services. There has been a marked increase in students with disabilities applying, entering and making their needs known in higher education.

The third tranche of HEFCE funding is aimed at improving the quality of provision, with an emphasis on collaboration across the sector as well as with outside bodies. To win bids for this funding institutions were required to demonstrate that the developments would be embedded within their provision and supported by them beyond the three years. It will be in the new millennium that these projects finally report on their achievements.

As a result of Dearing's recommendations there is to be parity of funding for full-time and part-time patterns of study, which will benefit many disabled students for whom part-time study is the preferred option. In addition, students who are not eligible for a maintenance grant will, from next year, be considered for the DSA. These initiatives, taken together, point to changes happening in the sector that will facilitate access to higher education for students with a range of learning needs. However, it is also clear that there is still much that remains to be done.

New Millennium - New deal?

As a result of the advances made in recent years those institutions which have done most to promote access have become more aware of the barriers and keys to equality of access to learning. Considerations of physical access to the learning environment and identification of central support services, together with staff awareness of disability issues, provide a good foundation upon which to radically challenge much that is taken for granted in higher education.

If disabled students are to be fully included in higher education then it is necessary to ensure that they have access to the full experience in HE. Presently many students find that this is circumscribed by limited support. One applicant to UEL required substantial modification to the residential accommodation to enable him to live on site. After identifying the extent of changes required, the Social Services refused to fully fund them. He is now attending as a day student and travelling several hours daily from home. Originally, the Social Services also refused to fund personal care to assist his lunch-time use of the toilet, suggesting that he could, instead, wear incontinence pads. The student contacted his local Member of Parliament about this decision, who managed to ensure that it was overturned.

Access to extra-curricular activities is also made more difficult for disabled students who rely on local authority transport services to get on and off campus. The service rarely operates outside of circumscribed times and students are constrained by the lack of flexibility in such arrangements. Presently questions of transport and extra-curricula activities remain outside the scope of consideration of most HEIs. Students are expected to be responsible for making their own arrangements for such matters. In such circumstances students are denied access to the kind of extra-curricula activities which are recognised to be part of the undergraduate experience.

The DSA mechanism, which makes funds available directly to the student, offers some freedom for the student to purchase the support which best meets their needs. However, it also places an additional burden on disabled students who must manage the purchase and maintenance of suitable equipment, as well as the recruitment, employment and payment of staff to support their learning needs. Some institutions offer support for students in accessing the DSA and managing the additional responsibilities that come with it, but presently no requirement is placed on HEIs to make any kind of accommodation for disability because of the sector's historical imperative of 'academic freedom'.

This is in contrast to the situation in the United States of America where institutions must, under the requirements of the Americans with Disabilities Act (1990), '... make reasonable accommodations in programs and activities' in order to provide equal access to qualified persons with disabilities (University of Georgia, 1997). This '...includes the whole scope of the institution's activities, including facilities, programs, and employment' (University of North Dakota, 1997), and according to Milani (1996, p.989) is:

> based on the premise that disability is a natural part of the human experience and in no way diminishes the rights of individuals to live independently, pursue meaningful careers, and enjoy full inclusion in the economic, political, cultural and educational mainstream of American society.

Whilst the rights of disabled students in the United States are enshrined in law, the legislation is vague about how far universities must go to accommodate students. Nevertheless, a number of court decisions have begun to clarify rights and responsibilities so that students know what to expect and institutions are more aware of what they must provide. In the United Kingdom disabled students have no such rights. The assumption, by senior managers and government, of a 'traditional' client group creates 'deviant' students; that is those for whom extra or additional accommodations must be made. Acceptance of a wider constituent group of students will need to be supported by a number of changes including flexible entry requirements, flexible learning outcomes, and increased student support and guidance.

Questions of pedagogy/androgogy are also crucial for widening participation in higher education. In recent years lecturers have been made aware that the curriculum content is biased and does not reflect the experience and/or concerns of those students who have historically been excluded from the higher education experience, including women, black and working class students. In some institutions additional courses have been introduced to try and accommodate these criticisms, for example women's studies and third world studies. This add-on approach has done little to challenge the mainstream curriculum, or to meet the demands of students. However, it is clear that introducing courses on disability will not meet the diverse needs of disabled students at university.

Accommodating disability issues in the higher education curriculum can only be achieved by a re-consideration of teaching methods and learning outcomes. Staff will find it necessary to be explicit about the criteria that they use for access to a course of study and for achievement of qualifications, and to justify any lack of flexibility in such arrangements. For example, students with specific learning disabilities such as dyslexia, are not generally admitted to teacher training courses and, at some universities, dyslexic students have been counselled not to pursue studies in languages. The assumption seems to be that these student will be unable to cope with the demands of reading and writing, despite examples which demonstrate the contrary.

Another example of staff developing specific admissions criteria for disabled students, concerns a student who experiences occasional and unpredictable loss of consciousness for short periods. She has been permitted to continue with the practical elements of her science degree, at her university, only after meeting several conditions specified by the Head of Department. The student has lived with, and managed, this condition with the co-operation of staff at school and FE prior to coming to university. She is now required to put in writing that she will not hold the university responsible for any injury or damage she may suffer; to get her medical consultant to specify a standard procedure for staff to follow if and when she loses consciousness, and to employ a personal assistant trained in first aid to attend practical classes and manage her recovery should she lose consciousness. Finally, there is the case of a blind student being refused entrance to a subject because the tutor described his teaching method as 'very visual', and himself not open to change because of pressures on his time.

The move to specify learning outcomes can be enabling, but if they are not used consistently and explicitly their use can, in some circumstances, be disabling. A student in the final year of a Business Studies degree, for example, was required to make a group presentation as part of his assessed work. The fact that the student's communication impairment made this impossible was not identified by tutors until year three. After identification of the exact skills which were to be demonstrated it was agreed that the student could plan and manage a presentation to be carried out by others and thus meet the course requirement. Ideally the admissions process should be such that it is not possible for a student to be admitted to a course where completion requires skills they cannot demonstrate or develop.

To accommodate disability issues in HE there will need to be more emphasis on the quality of teaching and learning, so that staff are encouraged to consider whether their teaching methods match the learning styles of diverse groups of students and how they can match this diversity. Recent emphasis on group project work and experiential learning whilst generally valuable, may be found to disadvantage some deaf and hearing impaired students. In one of the first year classes a hearing impaired student was unable to fully participate in small group discussion because the class environment was noisy, and the light was not sufficiently good to enable him to lip-read. He did manage to secure the services of a lip speaking communicator, which made the group work experience less stressful for him, but which acted as a barrier between him and the other group members. He needed to focus his attention on the communicator and, despite being given guidelines on how to work with a communicator, the other students still tended to talk to the communicator rather than to the student. In another example, a hearing impaired student on a counselling course was unable to participate in a simulation that required students to communicate whilst sitting back-to-back. This student also experienced difficulties with group discussions. In this case it was decided that she should raise a red flag when she could not detect the source of speech. Whilst this may have helped the group the student felt somewhat stigmatised by the procedure.

Although some teaching staff in HE do consider ways in which their teaching style can affect widening participation this is often at the expense of their own academic careers. Little credit is given in the sector to developing expertise in teaching. Those members of staff who are most highly regarded are those who generate income via the research assessment exercise (RAE). Thus, those staff who concentrate their energies on research and publishing are the most highly valued and those who direct their energies into teaching and supporting students are effectively penalised.

Quality teaching is the key to inclusion in HE, and this cannot yet be substituted by the use of individual resource based learning. The growing emphasis on the use of information technology benefits some students, but it is not yet of universal benefit. For example, the heavy reliance on the Windows environment causes difficulties for students who are blind. Visually impaired students and others who require enlarged print or alternative formats also find that, where these are available, extra time and costs are incurred. For students with certain physical and/or sensory disabilities, inappropriate seating and lighting at the IT workstations on campus, in laboratories, libraries and workshops, can also present difficulties- all difficulties which can be overcome with sufficient awareness and appropriate resources, but which presently remain problematic.

Conclusion

The above examples and discussion indicate much has been achieved in the last decade to facilitate the entry of students with disabilities into higher education. But what about inclusion? Much work remains to be done before it can be said with confidence that there is the beginning of including students with disabilities into the full higher education experience. To achieve this means finding new and innovative ways to fund support so that students can access the whole curriculum as well as the full range of extra-curricular activities; carrying out research into the ways in which a variety of teaching methods impact upon the learning experiences of different groups of students; and encouraging institutions to re-consider entry requirements and learning outcomes so that they are sufficiently flexible to accommodate students with disabilities. If the new millennium begins with us asking the right questions about the barriers to full inclusion, listening to the voices of disabled students and their representative organisations, and making honest efforts to reduce and remove the barriers, then there will be progress in some way of addressing equality in the twenty-first century. Also, the rights of disabled individuals have to be enshrined in legislation. Without the protection of the law it is likely that provision for disabled students in higher education will remain ad-hoc and patchy.

Bibliography

Aune, B.(1998), 'Higher Education and Disability in the United States of America: The Context, a Comprehensive Model, and Current Issues', in Hurst, A. (ed), *Higher Education and Disabilities: International Approaches*, Ashgate, Aldershot, UK.

Blunkett, D. (1997), *Higher Education for the 21st Century*, DfEE, London (web site: http://www.open.gov.uk/dfee/highed/foreword.html).

Disability on the Agenda (1995), *A Brief Guide to the Disability Discrimination Act*, DL40, London, UK.

DISinHE (1998), *Teaching Everyone, Disability and New Technology, a Guide for Lecturers*, SEARCH-ED Project, University of Dundee, UK.

Higher Education Information Service Trust (1998), *Disability Statements, a Guide to Good Practice*, Higher Education Funding Council for England, UK.

Highe Education Funding Council of England (1996), *Widening Access to Higher Education, A Report by the HEFCE's Advisory Group on Access and Participation*, HEFCE, London.

Higher Education Funding Council for England, (1996a), *Proposed Specification for Disability Statements to be Required from Institutions*, Circular 3/96, HEFCE, London.

Higher Education Funding Council for England (1996b), *Access to Higher Education: Students with Learning Difficulties and Disabilities*. A report on the 1993/94 and 1994/95 HEFCE special initiatives to encourage widening participation for students with disabilities, HEFCE, London.

Higher Education Statistics Agency (1997), *Research Datapack 5, Students with Disabilities 1995/96*, HESA, Glos., UK.

Hurst, A. (1999), 'The Dearing Report and Students with Disabilities and Learning Difficulties', in *Disability and Society*, vol.4, no.1, pp.65-85.

Institute for Learning and Teaching (1999), *Proposals for the National Framework for Higher Education Teaching*, paper presented for discussion at a meeting of the Staff and Educational Development Association, 11 March, London.

Milani, A.A. (1996), 'Disabled Students in Higher Education', in *Journal of College and University Law*, pp. 989-1043.

O'Hanlon, C. and Manning, J. (1994), Students with Disabilities: Applications to Higher Education, in *Educare*, Issue 50, pp. 30-31, Skill, London.

Petrie, H. and Gill, J. (1993), 'Current Research on Graphical User Interfaces for Visually Disabled Computer users', in *European Journal of Special Needs Education*, vol. 8, no. 2, pp. 153-8.

Robertson, D. and Hillman, J. (1997), 'Widening Participation in Higher Education for Students from Lower Socio-economic Groups and Students with Disabilities', Report 6 to Dearing, R. (1997), *Education in the Learning Society*. The Report of the National Committee of Inquiry into Higher Education, Stationery Office, London.

Segal Quince Wickstead (1999), *Guidance on Base-level Provision for Disabled Students in Higher Education Institutions*, A Report to HEFCE and HEFCW, SQW, Cambridge, UK.

Shaw, J. (1998), 'A Fair Go- the Impact of the Disability Discrimination Act (1992) on Tertiary Education in Australia', in Hurst, A. (ed), *Higher Education and Disabilities: Interntational Approaches*, Ashgate, Aldershot, UK.

University of Georgia (1997), brochure no title, The Office of Disability Services, University of Georgia (web site http://iris.dissvcs.uga.edu/~web/teaching.html).

University of North Dakota (1996), *Americans with Disabilities Act: The Law and its Impact on Post Secondary Education*, Disability Support Services, University of North Dakota (web site: http://www.und.nodak.edu/dept.dss/adalaw.html).

9 Enhancing Opportunities for Disabled Students: Comparisons across the Atlantic

MIRANDA PRESTON AND JENNIE GORBOLD

Abstract

Recent developments in the United Kingdom are indicators of a greater number of students with disabilities in higher education. However, there are many areas where further developments need to take place. In the last chapter Myers and Parker analysed the current state of play in the United Kingdom. In the United States, the situation for students with disabilities has been buoyant for some time. This chapter details the ways in which legislation there is more comprehensive, especially in that mental as well as physical disabilities are covered. Major concerns in the United States range from employers feeling they may be forced to hire 'murderous lunatics', the discerning of 'unseen' learning difficulties, to the view that learning disabilities are an invention of the middle classes that cannot accept their children being average.

The amount of money being spent by the Federal Government on the 'learning disability industry' necessitates questioning the disability culture that is perceived as encouraging students to focus on their weaknesses rather than their strengths. Perhaps even more worrying is the mis-match between education establishments where students with learning disabilities may get a lot of support, and places of employment where disabled people are not welcome, despite their qualifications.

The new millennium should not only see a proper implementation of current legislation in Britain, but use the examples from the United States to make wider the framework within which students with disability are seen. Otherwise new developments could remain tokenistic.

Introduction

During the 1980s, a considerable expansion in the uptake of higher education occurred in the United Kingdom, increasing numbers of both traditional and non-traditional groups. Improvements in identification, assessment and provision for special educational needs at school level have led to an increase in these kinds of students in higher education. The Disability Discrimination Act (1995), the requirement for disability statements in higher education and the Dearing Report (1997) have focused on the need for changes in the admission, assessment and provision for students with disabilities in Higher Education (HE). However, there is cause for concern regarding the long-term implications of these developments. This chapter highlights recent events in the United States related to these issues, and assesses the possibility of a similar situation developing in Britain.

The Current Situation in the United State of America

In the United States the situation for students with disabilities has been buoyant for some time. A series of legislative acts enshrined the rights of those with disabilities in law. The statutory framework for modern disability law was established in the Rehabilitation Act (1973) that set down what assistance disabled people would get in federal (central government) facilities. In this act, a learning disability defined as:

> a disorder in one or more of the basic psychological processes involved in using language, spoken or written (which may manifest itself in imperfect ability to listen, think, speak, write, spell or do mathematical calculations.

This broad definition is echoed in all subsequent disability legislation, especially the Americans with Disabilities Act (1975) that mandated an array of services for disabled public school students. The 1990 Americans with Disabilities Act (ADA) extended the protection of the Rehabilitation Act into the private sector. All three laws are quite vague as to how people with disabilities must be treated. As the ADA puts it, in the case of any individual possessing a 'disability' that results in 'substantial impairment' of a 'major life activity', schools and employers cannot 'discriminate' and must provide 'reasonable accommodation'. The Equal Employment Opportunity Commission's announcement that the ADA covers not only physically, but mentally handicapped individuals has attracted a great deal of publicity.

Nightmare scenarios of employers being forced to hire 'murderous lunatics' are being discussed. The issue of an unseen learning difficulty is a more subtle one, but one that is having a profound effect on higher education establishments in the United States.

However, many are very sceptical of the focus on students with special needs. Farkes (1997) wondered:

> why students who cannot learn or pay attention should be admitted to college. Do we train people who cannot walk to be tennis players or people who cannot see to become painters? Many colleges are suffering from financial malnutrition and are compelled to relax their admissions standards. They often admit students with 'learning disabilities' and give them privileges that other students do not have. Some might graduate, but then what? Will graduate schools also welcome them? And if they graduate, will they find work? Would anyone want to seek the services of doctors or lawyers with attention deficit disorder?

Defining Disability Down

Ten students with learning disabilities filed action against Jon Westling, the provost of Boston University (BU) (USA, 1997). Westling had taken an aggressive approach to BU's Office of Learning Disabilities Support. In June and July 1995 Westling made speeches denouncing the 'zealous advocacy' of the learning disabilities movement. His dominant theme was that:

> the learning disability movement is a great mortuary for the ethics of hard work, individual responsibility, and pursuit of excellence, and also for genuinely humane social order.

Westling described a learning disabled student whom he called 'Somnolent Samantha'. He explained that she had a learning disability in the area of auditory processing, a nod would need the following accommodations:

> Time and a half on all quizzes, tests and examinations, double time on any mid-term or final examinations; examinations in a room separate from other students; copies of my lecture notes; and a seat at the front of the class. Samantha...might fall asleep in my class, and I should be particularly concerned to fill her in on any material she missed while dozing.

Westling fabricated the student named Samantha in order to reinforce his point regarding students with learning disabilities. He later admitted not only that no such student existed, but that she really did not even represent a prototype of the learning disabled students he had encountered. The result was that Wrestling stepped up requirements for documentation and waivers for exemptions from maths and foreign language requirements. The date of the court case was July 1996, and the award was made in the students' favour a year later. They were awarded a total of thirty thousand dollars.

An Invention of the Middle Classes?

This decision caused a storm of controversy in the United States and a flurry of articles appeared in leading journals and newspapers. In 'Defining Disability Down', Shalet (1997) rubbished the increase in both the variety of learning disabilities being discovered, and the increase in the numbers of students being identified. She propounded the view that learning disabilities were an invention of the middle classes that could not stand the prospect of their offspring being average:

> In prosperous sun-dappled school districts around the country, exotic new learning disabilities are popping up, each requiring its own costly cure. In Orange County where 'executive function disorder' (difficulty in initiating, organising and planning behaviour) reigns, parents have begun demanding that schools foot the bill for horseback riding lessons.

Peter Hartman, Superintendent of the Saddleback Unified School District, felt that (Shalet, 1997):

> such attitudes were becoming common and the problem seemed to be less inattentive children than over attentive parents, many of whom were unwilling to believe that their progeny was less than perfect.

This article sparked a strong response from those on both sides of the debate. The learning disabled fought back. Alexander (1997) was clear about his views as someone who had a learning disability, he was given double time in college, the option of either doing class exams on computer or taking double time to make his handwriting somewhat legible. He did not feel that minor compensations were either unreasonable or unfair. In an incredible demonstration of ignorance,

Shalet was actually challenging the very existence of learning disabilities. As a result, people with learning difficulties and their advocates, were presented as (Shalet, 1997) 'fanatics, poor students, lazy students or ambitious cheats'.

Disability Culture - Disabling Culture?

In the same correspondence page as Shalet's letter, Reddall (1997) presented the opposing point of view:

> Ruth Shalet's 'Defining Disability Down' is chilling in its implications when the phonologically challenged law student who has received preferential treatment throughout her academic career, is refused employment by the law firm to which she applies, she may well sue them for discrimination against the learning disable. After all, it's got to be somebody's faulty that she can't get hired. This should not surprise us; it was the psychiatric industry that recently redefined coffee drinking, playing video games, clumsiness, and yes, snaring, as mental disorders. It is a small step to reduce laziness and stupidity to pathology as well.

Robert Sternber (1997), a Professor of Psychology and Education at Yale, also questioned the rapid rise of the learning disability industry, which at present costs the Federal Government around 3.25 billion dollars per year. Thus prevailing learning disability culture appeared to be encouraging students to focus on their weakness rather than their strengths. The scene that was set for failure later on (Sternber, 1997):

> Though some students who receive generous accommodations for learning disabilities may gain in the short run, with improved grades and test scores, the long-term implications can be disturbing. Such students may simply not be able to handle that they have been able to enter with the extra assistance they have received. Indeed, the saddest aspect of the fixation with entitlements is that, while helping these students succeed in school, we are setting them up for possible failure later on. Our society has created a cult of self-esteem in which we make it hard for children to fail. But there are great advantages to failing. That is how we learn to correct our weaknesses. And that, in turn, is one of the first steps to success.

This article provoked a strong response, with parents of children with special needs fighting back. One respondent was a special education teacher and the parent of three children, one of whom had learning disabilities. She was dismayed at Sternber's approach and had yet to meet parents who were overjoyed when their children were diagnosed with learning disabilities and thus eligible for testing modifications, tutoring and exemptions from certain subjects. She believed that (Benjamin, 1997):

> if students need to learn the difference between living with a disability and using it as an excuse, that's the job of teachers and those who train teachers. None of this justifies attempts to deny students the help they need. Mr Sternberg would prefer the learning disabled take the more traditional path of smart children who cannot succeed in school: dropout drug dealers, gang leaders and criminals.

The Way Forward for Britain

The United States appears to have a more open public debate about attitudes and provision for disability. However recent court cases may be a part of similar developments in the United Kingdom. One example is that of Pamela Phelps.

In 1997 Phelps was awarded £45,00.00 against the London Borough of Hillingdon for failing to identify and provide for her dyslexia, leaving her educationally unable to fulfil her potential in the workplace. She had mistakenly been assessed by education psychologist Diane Melling as having 'emotional problems' rather than dyslexia. Although an appeal by Hillingdon was upheld, this case may be the beginning of rights of disabled being taken seriously in the United Kingdom. The judge, Mr Justice Garland, laid the blame firmly at the feet of the psychologist:

> This was more than an error of judgement: it was a failure to exercise the degree of care and skill to be expected of an ordinarily competent member of her profession.

Higher education institutions, related funding and quality control bodies, such as Higher Education Funding Council (HEFCE), organisations concerned about the quality of teaching such as the new Institute for Learning and Teaching in Higher Education, need to have comprehensive, effective policies to ensure adequate dignity and scope for students with disability. As with the policy adopted by the Teacher Training Agency in Britain, quality assessment should include employment of students with disability. Increasing the number of under-represented groups, such as men in primary schools, minority ethnic groups and people with disability has been a key target for the Teacher Training Agency.

Good practice includes the publication by higher education institutions of comprehensive disability handbooks. These give details of all resources and concession available to this group of students, so that they can make informed choices. A disability statement should also influence a clear, non-discriminatory admissions policy, and adequate access to supportive technology, specialised study skills, and examination concessions which together should form a web of support. As the process of accessing disability funding is currently changing, it seems likely that funding will go directly to institutions, rather than to individual students. The authors feel that the current system (individual disability grants administered and provided by the LEAD), whilst benefiting many deserving students, is open to lack of consistency and some abuse. A national system applied fairly and consistently to all disabled students, through their own institutions, would ensure that no one was disadvantaged.

Equal opportunities can only truly exist for disabled students when national directives have filtered down to an institutional level, and influenced admissions, examination concessions, access to supportive technology, specialised study skills and ongoing appropriate staff development. The cases in the United States listed in this chapter, linked to a similar trend that has been noted in the United Kingdom, underlines the need for strong national guidelines in order to protect both students and institutions in the future.

Bibliography

Benjamin, C. (1997), *Sunday New York Times*, letter, August 25, Brooklyn.
Dearing, R. (1997), *Higher Education in the Learning Society,* **Report of The National Committee for the Enquiry into Higher Education**, Stationery Office, London.
Farkas, T. (1997), *Sunday New York Times*, letter, August 25, New York.
Hartman, P. (1997), *The New York Republic*, 6.10.97, letter.
Reddall, D. (1997), *The New York Republic,* letter, October 6, North Toro, Massacheusetts.
Shalet, R. (1997), 'Defining Disability Down', in *The New York Republic*, August 25.
Simon, Alexander (1997), *The New York Republic,* letter, October 6, Stamford, Connecticut.
Smith, S. (1992), *Succeeding Against the Odds*, Tarcher, Parigee, New York.
Sternberg, R. (1997), *The New York Times*, letter, October 6.

USA (1997), *Lexis 12727*, US Dist.(08.97), Report on the findings of Students vs. Boston University (Law and Order judgment).
Vail, P. (1990), *About Dyslexia: Unraveling the Myth*, Rosemont, New Jersey.
Westman, J. (1990), *Handbook for Learning Disabilities*, Allyn and Bacon, Boston.

10 The Role of the Student Counselling Service in the Promotion of Equal Opportunities in Education in the New Millennium

RUTH CALEB AND HEIDI GILHOOLY

Abstract

As increasing numbers of students enter higher education, the role of student counselling services needs to evolve and develop to meet the needs of all students. These have changed, and the severity of mental difficulties has increased in the past few years. There is a trend towards increasing proportions of students being severely disturbed. There is concern at the rising number of students of all ethnicities attending higher education counselling services with severe mental difficulties and that the majority of counsellors are white, and they come from what may loosely be termed, a relatively middle-class background. Ethnic minority students are under-represented in number amongst students using student counselling services.

These factors, and the realisation of the important role that the student counselling service plays in supporting the individual student through emotional and psychological difficulties, led one university counselling service to the view that intrinsic changes were necessary. This chapter explores the ways the particular student counselling service evolved actively to offer a service based on student need and equal opportunity, and describes the recruitment of a multi-cultural staff team, the embracing of the differences within team members, the acknowledgement of student needs and ways of working with ethnic and cultural differences within the counselling process. This approach for determining effective support for all categories of students needs to be taken seriously.

Introduction

As increasing numbers of students enter into higher education, the role of student counselling services needs to evolve and develop to meet the needs of all students. The former Association of Student Counselling, now renamed the Association for University and College Counsellors, which is the professional organisation for student counsellors, has indicated through its surveys that needs of students have changed, and that the severity of mental difficulties has increased in the past few years. In the Association of Student Counselling's 1995-1996 survey of counselling services in Further and Higher Education, the trend is demonstrated towards increasing proportions of severely disturbed students - 63 per cent of institutions surveyed reported an increase in psychological disturbance among their clients and less than 1 per cent said it had decreased (Phippen, 1997). The Heads of University Counselling Services (HUCS), and other higher education groups have expressed concerns at the rising number of students of all ethnicities attending higher education counselling services with severe mental difficulties.[1] The HUCS report, Degrees of Disturbance: the New Agenda, explores the roles of the educational context, the widening of access to higher education, societal shifts and changing community resources and health provision in the growth of mental health problems in students.

The Association for University and College Counsellors has not collected data about the ethnic composition of student counsellors, although there is a general awareness that the majority of counsellors are white, come from what may loosely be termed, a relatively middle-class background.[2] It is perhaps thus not surprising that ethnic minority students are under-represented amongst students using student counselling services - again, this is another area where no firm national statistics seem to be available.

These factors, and the realisation of the important role that the student counselling service plays in supporting the individual student through emotional and psychological difficulties, determined the view of Thames Valley University Student Counselling Service that intrinsic changes were necessary. The need for the service to evolve arose particularly in view of the Mission Statement[3] supporting mass participation in higher education as a contribution to equality and social justice, and also the Equal Opportunities Policy[4] which denounces discriminatory attitudes and is committed to a programme of action to eradicate discrimination and inequality - of particular importance in 1997, European Year Against Racism.

The Role of the Student Counselling Service

This chapter explores the way the Thames Valley University Student Counselling Service actively evolved a service based on student need and equal opportunity, and describes the recruitment of a multicultural staff team, the embracing of the differences within team members, the acknowledgement of student need and ways of working with ethnic and cultural differences within the counselling process.

University Profile

In the academic year of 1996/1997, Thames Valley University (TVU) had 10,868 students, of whom 35 per cent were full-time and 65 per cent were part-time. Furthermore, of the full-time students, 63 per cent were female and 41 per cent were from ethnic minority groups.[5] Yet based on previous years' experience, it could be predicted that most users of the counselling services would be white women.

On the main university site in Ealing, in 1994/1995, 76 per cent of clients attending the Student Counselling Service were white, 24 per cent were from ethnic minorities, of which 12 per cent were Asian. In 1995/1996, over 50 per cent of clients were white, 14 per cent were Asian and 30 per cent were from other ethnic minorities. However, 1996/1997 proved quite different. Of the clients attending the counselling service, 32 per cent were white, 68 per cent were from ethnic minorities, 43 per cent being of Asian background.[6] This trend proved to be ongoing; in 1997/1998 when 33 per cent of clients were white and 61 per cent were from ethnic minorities, 43 per cent being of Asian background.

How was this Change Possible?

Recruitment of a Multicultural Staff Team

Rose (1999) details the need to recruit counsellors from ethnic minorities, whilst outlining the dangers therein. At the end of the academic year in June 1993, at TVU there were four part-time white counsellors, and the service may well have been perceived as eurocentric. By the beginning of the new academic year in October 1993, three of those counsellors had left and three new ones had been recruited. The recruitment process ensured that the University Equal Opportunity Policy had been implemented. By luck, skill, unconscious positive discrimination or a mixture of all three, the new counsellors brought with them their own experiences of Indian,

Asian and European backgrounds and the Senior Counsellor was the only counsellor for whom English was a first language.

By 1997, the service was well known for being multi-ethnic, all four counsellors coming from different ethnic, cultural and religious minorities, who had much to learn from each other, particularly about customs, beliefs and family and community structures that were unfamiliar to them.

Working with the Differences in the Team

One of the first tasks taken on by the new counselling team was the formulation of a Student Counselling Service Equal Opportunities and Counselling Policy committing us to the intention not to impose our own culture on clients. Thus began the process of raising our assumptions about our own and each others' cultures and owning them. Rose (1997) has pointed out the importance of acknowledging the difference and not denying the issue in the belief that racial awareness is synonymous with the denial of difference as an issue - 'Colour doesn't make any difference to me' or 'I've got black friends'.

At the beginning of the time together as a staff team there was perhaps an assumption made by some of the administrative staff booking appointments that clients would prefer to see a counsellor from their own ethnic or cultural group. This came to light as an issue after a particular case which meant that the counsellors themselves had to get to grips with the issue of difference.

Case Study

An Asian man asked to see a counsellor. He was asked by the administrative staff who was booking appointments, which counsellor he wished to see; when he asked who the counsellors were, he was told that there was an Asian, a Thai, a Spanish and a Jewish counsellor. He chose the Asian. During his appointment he explained that he was the father of a female student who had left home, and that he wanted the counsellor to locate his daughter and persuade her to return home, saying 'as an Asian woman it is your duty'. He believed that she should understand and collude with his position. When told that what he had asked for would not be possible, he left the counselling room angry and disappointed. The counsellor had understood his feelings from her own sense of family within her culture and was left feeling uncomfortable, but remained certain of her professional code of practice and duty as a counsellor to keep confidentiality for the students at the university.

This case opened a discussion about the need to train reception staff, and about assumptions around our different ethnicities and the assumed collusion that might occur if a client chose a counsellor by ethnicity alone. It became clear that a client might choose a counsellor of different ethnicity, especially if there is internalised racism, causing a black client to believe that the white counsellor might be superior to the black. Kareem (1992), who founded the NAFSIYAT Intercultural Therapy Centre, agreed that matching clients to counsellors by culture may diminish the human element. Another important factor to be taken into consideration is the danger that in a multicultural organisation, counsellors from ethnic minorities may feel obliged to take on the responsibility for clients from ethnic minorities, and as Rose (1997) discusses, causing white counsellors to deny the existence of black clients in terms of a direct counselling relationship.

The development of the staff as a team came to depend on the raising of issues that were at times uncomfortable, especially as the senior counsellor happened to be white. It was facilitated by an atmosphere of trust, the empowerment of each counsellor and the cascading of skills and particular expertise by each counsellor through internal development workshops.

Acknowledging Student Need

On examining the statistics of the student body it became clear that certain groups, for example white female students aged 21 and under, were using the Student Counselling Service, but other groups were hardly using the service at all. There was the recognition of the fact that the needs of the total student population were not being fully addressed.

Thames Valley University's largest campus is in Ealing, close to the heart of a large Asian community. One outstanding group that was preponderant in the university but the service did not seem to be reaching was Asian female students living at home. The Student Counselling Team were aware that this group might have particular issues to face which might mean that they would find it difficult to find their way to the counselling service, due to physical factors such as the presence of chaperones and curfews, and emotional elements such as fear or a sense of disloyalty to the family.

Having a multi-cultural Student Counselling Team would not be enough in itself to attract this clientele. Other initiatives included:

- Multicultural posters to publicise the Student Counselling Service;
- Connections made with the Student Union and the Asian Society;

- Links forged with community organisations; joint initiatives were offered, including a drop-in workshop run with Southall Black Sisters which, though it did not attract a large number of students, did publicise the willingness of the Student Counselling Service to hear and acknowledge the specific issues that Asian women may have issues such as the difficulty of belonging to both Asian and Western cultures, to having their freedom restricted by curfews or chaperones, and problems with relationships;
- A list of referral agencies compiled for those clients who felt their needs would be better met by an organisation specialising in the client's own culture;
- Workshops offered for university staff, titled 'Embracing the Difference' which allowed the opportunity for staff to explore the impact that individual difference made in their work with students, and to examine their own cultural meanings including 'being white'.

Aisha Dupont - Joshua (1996) has suggested that white counsellors must look at what their own culture of being white means, which in the video 'Being White', is understood by the white people interviewed as 'being normal'. She states that black people are not abnormal but different. Yet the very term 'different' implies a norm from which others differ. It is necessary to understand that people are all 'different' to one another, with unique backgrounds and experiences.

The Counselling Process - Working with Difference

Many assume that awareness of equal opportunities and antiracism can be taught at workshops and courses. It is, of course, crucial to have an interest in other cultures and to learn about the rituals and traditions of various religions and cultures. There may be differing cultural - and individual - expectations of what counselling means, and it is important to offer an assessment interview in which expectations and goals may be explored before counselling itself begins.

Ongoing training in cultural issues for all staff in education is crucial. But the Thames Valley University Student Counselling Team has concluded that working with human difference effectively is not merely learned by having a basic awareness of the rites and rituals of different cultures and ethnic groups. Multicultural counselling does not necessarily involve changing working practice; it stems from an attitude of mind, and a wish to understand what their culture, race, religion and sexuality mean to those individuals so the clients can be helped to explore their world. It means not being afraid of one's own ignorance of culture.

No-one can know about all cultures and even if it were possible, there would be a danger of making assumptions about the way of life of an individual. As Eleptheriadou (1992, pp. 23-24) points out:

> If the client is perceived as representing a certain culture the danger is that the complexity and uniqueness of the individual's own learning and experience is undervalued and stereotyping and prejudice may be the end product. It is important to remember that the client will eventually provide the counsellor with all the cultural information that is necessary and relevant to the therapy.

The TVU Student Counselling Service noted that the problems raised by the young Asian women clients differed on the whole from the presenting issues of the general student population, focusing on cultural expectations, the problems of an extended family relationships including sexual abuse. For the many final year students who attended, the particular issue was how to fit back into family patterns when no longer a student, especially in terms of ambivalence towardsa proposed arranged marriage. These were by no means issues for every client, but the issues were generalised enough to show that the perception of staff that this client group had particular needs was vindicated.

The Service realised that if challenged by a client that the staff could not understand, for example, the experience of being black, it was far better to accept one's own lack of knowledge, voice it, and ask what the experience of being black means to that client. Dupont - Joshua (1996) sees this approach as empowering for the client, leveling out the imbalance of power between counsellor and client. Students who came to the Student Counselling Service at TVU were able to work on their problems with a counsellor, whether of the same ethnic background or not, who respected the student's experience although they may not have been fully conversant in it. Many students who came to counselling with issues relating to conflicts reported having had a positive experience of working on their difficulties in their evaluation sheets.[7]

The following are extracts from a client's letter:

> I've finally managed to put pen to paper and have filled out the evaluation form. I've written loads but still couldn't bring across how much you have changed my life ...

About two years ago I went to my GP with the same 'symptoms' of anxiety, he didn't think twice about putting me on beta-blockers (which I threw away) to 'reduce my anxiety ...

I came to you as a 'last resort'. I felt the establishment had pigeon-holed this young black girl but what choice did I have? and I was very cynical about counselling etc. I sincerely believe that without counselling I would have been on some form of medication.

I know that as a black woman, the odds are stacked against me. I can't afford to loose my mind! You didn't assume anything about me, or categorise me or pigeon-hole me.

I've experienced so-called educated people treat me like nothing because of the colour of my skin, and I took a chance ... I will always be endebted to you for your time and patience but mostly for accepting me as I am.

Conclusion

This chapter has shown how Thames Valley University was able to meet more of the needs of its particular student population by the recruitment of a multicultural counselling team, by processing the cultural and ethnic differences within that team, through actively working with student needs and by putting their experience into the counselling process.

These methods are of even greater importance in the light of the Stephen Lawrence Inquiry Report (Macpherson, 1999) which concludes that racism exists within all organisations and institutions. The report expresses the need for radical thinking and sustained action to tackle overt and subtle discriminatory practices and attitudes. The role of education is emphasised in the prevention and addressing of discrimination, in order better to reflect the needs of a diverse society.

Student Counselling Services are of great importance not only for enhancing students' emotional well being but also for enabling them to concentrate on their studies and achieve their full academic and personal potential, helping them become a part of a multicultural community that forms a university. The role of a Student Counselling Service is to recognise its student profile and to ensure that the needs of all students are met in ways appropriate to their culture. It is suggested that the processes outlined, which are as dynamic and ever changing as the student population itself, and requiring constant evaluation, are successful as a way forward in the development of equal opportunities within an educational setting.

Notes

1   Heads of University Counselling Services meeting October 30, 1997.
2   Mark Phippen, Past Chair of the Association of Student Counselling, personal communication, June 1997.
3   The Thames Valley University Mission:
    'Thames Valley University supports mass participation in higher education as a contribution to equality and social justice. The University aims to become a student-driven institution, committed primarily to teaching and learning and playing a major part in the educational, cultural and economic life of the region. It will support these places by developing and sustaining partnershi with other organisations and providers in the public, private and voluntary sectors'.
4   The Thames Valley University Equal Opportunities Policy is as follows:

    Thames Valley University is committed to the value of achieving equality of opportunity for all students and staff in a learning environment free from discrimination on the basis of gender, race, age, social class, disability, sexuality or other characteristics which may give rise to unequal treatment.

    The University, whilst appreciating that the process of acquiring discriminatory attitudes are subtle and often unconscious, believes that such discrimination impoverishes the community by limiting horizons and restricting choices.

    The University recognises the power of education to challenge inequality and welcomes the positive contribution it can make to overcome discriminatory attitudes and behaviour in our society.

    The University recognises that passive support for equal opportunities is insufficient and is committed to a programme of action to ensure that equal opportunities are a reality for all and not simply an aspiration.
5   Thames Valley University Factfile for the academic year 1996/1997.
6   Thames Valley University Student Counselling Service Annual Report 1996/1997.
7   Evaluation sheets are given to all clients after counselling sessions and returned to the Student Counselling Service, anonymously if preferred. The are one of several methods of quality assurance sued by the Service.

Bibliography

Dupont-Joshua, A. (1996), 'Race, Culture and the Therapeutic Relationship: Working with Difference Creatively', in *Counselling*, August 1996, pp. 220-223.

Elephtheriadou, Z. (1992), 'Multi-Cultural Counselling and Psychotherapy: A Philosophical Framework', in *Psychologos: International Review of Psychology*, 3, 1992, pp. 21-29.

Kareem, J. (1992), 'The NAFSIYAT Inter-Cultural Therapy Centre', in Kareem J. and Littlewood, R. (eds.) *Intercultural Therapy*, Blackwell Scientific Publications, Oxford.

Macpherson, W. (1999), *The Stephen Lawrence Inquiry Report*, Stationery Office, London.

Okorocha, E. (1996), 'Cultural Clues to Student Guidance', in *The Times Higher Educational Supplement*, June 7.

Phippen, M. (1996), 'The 1995-6 Association for Student Counselling Survey of Counselling Services in Further and Higher Education', in *The Association for University and College Counsellors Newsletter and Journal*, November, pp. 11-20.

Rana, R., Smith, E. and Walkling, J. (1999), *Degrees of Disturbance: The New Agenda*, Heads of University Counselling Services Report, London.

Rose, E. (1997), 'Daring to Work with Internalised Racism', in *Counselling*, May, pp. 92-94.

11 Is Bilingualism an Obstacle to Inclusion for Deaf Children?

JOY JARVIS

Abstract

Certain educationists will be very familiar with the term 'bilingualism', a key area of concern in the field of education and cultural diversity; others will be focusing on deaf children, but mainly in the area generally called 'special needs'. This chapter shows why considering these two areas, generally treated separately, is fundamental to the quality of education received by a certain group of children. It also indicates how it is possible, and necessary, to widen the category of bilingualism by logically including a new one.

The deaf community is now identified as a linguistic minority, which gives a new meaning to the word bilingualism. For deaf children the use of British Sign Language (BSL) and English makes them bilingual. There are a number of issues surrounding bilingualism in terms of signed and spoken languages, in the education of deaf children. This chapter elaborates on the significance of BSL and the need to examine the range of issues affecting deaf children, other children at school, parents and teachers.

Underlying the discussion in this chapter are questions such as the complex implications of equality; for instance, including the deaf children in the mainstream classroom may in one respect be regarded as treating them as equal to other children, but it could in fact deprive them of the maximum opportunities they need for learning. It also raises much more forcefully than in the past in debates around bilingualism, the broader responsibilities arising from integration of a group of bilingual children in a school community. Consideration of bilingual children in the context of cultural diversity had normally been confined to the overall educational achievement of the bilingual children only.

Introduction

The purpose of this chapter is to explore some issues surrounding bilingualism, in terms of signed and spoken languages, in the education of deaf children. What is the meaning of bilingualism when it is applied to deaf children? Is bilingualism incompatible with inclusion? What are the needs of deaf children in the context of their entitlement to good education? It could be argued that a bilingual policy is not possible in an inclusion model based on local placement. Real inclusion, involving equal opportunities for linguistic and educational growth, may need to take place in area resourced provision. This has implications for educational services and schools and for our understanding of inclusive education.

Deaf Children and Bilingualism

Most children in the world, and some in Britain, grow up using more than one language. These languages will be used in different contexts and with different levels of facility. Their bilingualism will be generated by family and cultural situations and by where they are living at a particular time. For deaf children the situation is different. Bilingualism, involving the use of British Sign Language (BSL) and English, will be due to their hearing loss. Bouvet (1990) argues that deaf children are 'destined to become bilingual and bicultural', the argument being that children who are profoundly deaf will need, for ease of communication and for reasons of identity, to be part of the deaf community. This will involve the use of a signed language. In addition, in order to communicate with the hearing world, they will need to understand and use English in spoken and/or written form.

The Study of Sign Language

Baker (1997) suggests that 'sign language is the language of all deaf children'. This is based on the assumption that for profoundly deaf children who can hear a little, even with the most powerful hearing aids, their sense of vision will be used to learn language. They will learn language by eye rather than by ear. Until fairly recently an argument for having a spoken and not a signed language as a first language was based on the assumption that signed languages were 'inferior'. They did not have sophisticated structure and vocabulary and could not, therefore, be used by the child to develop cognitively as well as linguistically.

Research in the field of linguistics, however, has shown that signed languages have complex rule systems and have equal status in linguistic terms to spoke languages (Kyle and Woll, 1986). In addition, through the study of deaf children of deaf parents, it can be seen that these children go through the same processes of language acquisition in terms of learning communication skills, making over-generalizations and developing rule systems in signed language that hearing children do when acquiring spoken language. Deaf parents will also make similar adjustments to support their children's linguistic development as hearing parents will do by modifying and structuring the communicative context and their own input. Differences arise in relation to the modality rather than the approach. For example, while hearing parents may emphasize key words by intonation deaf parents may make signs slower or larger to support their child's learning (Harris, 1992).

Deaf Children and Deaf Parents

The underlying principles of languages, whether spoken or signed, and the process of acquisition of these languages appear to be the same. Deaf children of deaf parents may show better emotional adjustment and thinking skills than deaf children of hearing parents and one reason for this may be their understanding and use of their first language at an age appropriate time. (Marcshark, 1993). Other factors could include deaf parents' better adjustment to the diagnosis of deafness in their child and their understanding of interaction needs from birth. For deaf children of deaf parents, therefore, the linguistic argument for the acceptance of sign language as an appropriate language for communicating and learning validates their decision to bring their children up in what may well be their own first language. It is the language of the family. It is also the language of the deaf community. Ladd (1988) notes 'The deaf community can now be identified as a linguistic minority', rather than as handicapped people. The role of language in culture and in the development of identity and self esteem in an individual is important. Lawson (1981, p. 23) confirms:

> BSL is the native language of the deaf community in Britain and ... its usage is a powerful, cohesive bond resulting in unrestricted and relaxed exchanged of thought, ideas and feelings between members of the deaf community.

For deaf children of deaf parents, therefore, their development of one language at home and later meeting another language in the wider community and at school will be similar to the experiences of hearing children with a minority language as a first language.

Deaf Children and Hearing Parents

However, for the majority of deaf children this is not the case. Most deaf children have hearing parents: parents who may well have never communicated with a deaf adult and who know nothing about sign language. How could bilingualism work for these children? An argument could be that due to their hearing loss they will have difficulty developing a spoken language. Their language will, therefore, be very delayed and this could have significant developmental and educational implications. A child entering school at five, understanding and using a handful of words will clearly be at a grave disadvantage. If they use BSL at home, however, they can develop this as their first language through vision and come to school with an intact language as a basis for moving towards the acquisition of a second, spoken, language.

However, for parents to bring up their child in a language they do not themselves use is no mean feat and almost inevitably the child will receive limited input. How much language input one needs in order to acquire a first language is unclear and it would seem that children can develop linguistic rules based on fairly limited input, although children who meet BSL after the pre-school years are likely to become less sophisticated users of the language (Gallaway and Woll, 1994). If parents know and use little sign language, but are aiming to communicate through this mode, then it is likely that their deaf children will have limited first language ability by the time they reach school age. Other children may meet BSL for the first time when they get to school. In either case the role of the school is very different from its role in relation to hearing bilingual pupils. Rather than helping children to build a new language on the basis of one that is already established its role may well be to support the development of their pupils' first language.

Sign Language at School

Young deaf children, therefore, may need support in school to develop BSL as their first language. This implies that the school needs staff who are fluent BSL users and that BSL will be the mode of communication in the classroom. Deaf children with good sign language skills will also need BSL in the classroom as due to lack of hearing they will be unable to access the curriculum through spoken language. The British Deaf Association (1996, p.7) argues that prerequisites for the bilingual education of deaf children are:

(a) ... a bilingual environment where all staff recognize the importance of both languages and both cultures;
(b) ongoing deaf awareness in the school and for all professionals and staff;
(c) access to a deaf peer group;
(d) curriculum delivery and assessment in the child's preferred language;
(e) BSL and deaf studies curriculum;
(f) English curriculum based on modern foreign language curriculum;
(g) Interpreting support for deaf parents at meetings;
(h) Information about the school, etc. in BSL on video.

If these are accepted as the criteria for bilingual education for deaf children, the question that has to be answered is whether they are incompatible with inclusive education.

Inclusive Education and Deaf Children

The move towards inclusive education has been growing nationally and internationally during the past two decades. One example is the Green Paper (DfEE, 1997) which emphasizes the importance of including more children with special educational needs in mainstream schools. For many educationalists this means that all children should have the right to be placed in their local school with appropriate support. To do anything less is seen as a denial of human right. (Hall, 1997). The majority of deaf children are currently placed in mainstream schools and most of these will be educated orally. While many individuals will be successful, the overall picture is one of under-achievement in relation to hearing children (Powers, 1996). There are many arguments against placing individual deaf children in mainstream schools. They include problems with social integration due to communication difficulties between the deaf child and his/her hearing peers, problems with self-esteem when deaf children lack deaf role models, and lack of equal participation within the classroom and therefore limited access to the curriculum (Stimson and Lang, 1994). Baldwin (1994, p.165) believes that

> Full inclusion denies the deaf child access to an environment that addresses his/her unique social and emotional needs.

Another argument against full inclusion could be a bilingual policy. Conditions necessary for a bilingual approach to the education of deaf children include a deaf peer group. This would not be possible if children were individually integrated. Pickersgill (1997, p.18) states:

> individual deaf children in mainstream schools cannot be provided with sign bilingual support.

Bilingual education for deaf children and individual placement in mainstream schools would, therefore, appear to be incompatible. This does not mean that inclusion in a wider sense is not possible. As a minority group deaf children need the opportunity to be part of mainstream language and culture and to have opportunities of working and playing with hearing peers. However, if the educational provision is to be bilingual then clearly this inclusion will need to be inclusion in groups. Baldwin (1994, p.165) notes:

> there is much to be said for a critical mass of deaf children being enrolled within a single educational programme.

Deaf children, however, have been in units attached to mainstream schools for many years. What would be the difference with a bilingual inclusive programme?

Models of Provision

One approach from America is 'co-enrolment' (Kirchner, 1994). With this model co-enrolment classes were established at an elementary school. Deaf and hearing children were enrolled in these classes which had reduced numbers. Each class was taught by a team of a mainstream teacher and a teacher of the deaf (who may also have been deaf) and sign language and spoken English were both used as the languages of instruction. This gave the deaf pupils access to the curriculum, to deaf and hearing peers and opportunities to develop bilingually. Kirchner (1994, p.163) notes:

This strategy places deaf and hard of hearing students on an equal footing with their hearing peers instead of becoming merely 'foreign visitors' in the regular class.

Nearer to home, bilingual provision has been set up for deaf nursery aged children in Leeds (Knight 1997). The context is a nursery with 26 places for hearing children. Approximately 10 deaf children also attend the nursery. Staffing is enhanced by teachers of the deaf, deaf instructors and nursery nurses. The deaf children spend the morning together with specialist staff using both BSL and English. Lunch is taken together with staff who use the preferred language of the child to talk socially, while in the afternoon the deaf children are in the mainstream, many with support. Placement is flexible and can be mixed with placement for some of the time in the child's local nursery. Children are observed to see which language is emerging as their first language so that support can be given in that language. Plans are being made to provide two bases in the school, one using BSL and the other English so that children can move between the two as language preference emerges.

Pickersgill (1997) asserts that in a true bilingual model children may need access to a BSL dominant or an English dominant teaching approach but that all deaf children would be expected to use, to different extents, both languages. This mirrors hearing bilinguals' different uses and facility with their spoken languages. If this is to be the case then the use of a bilingual approach would lead to fewer individual placements of children in mainstream schools and more placements in groups with other deaf children.

Discussion

Bilingual education for deaf children could, therefore, be seen as an obstacle to inclusion if this is narrowly defined as individual placement within the local school. It could, however, be seen as enhancing inclusion if this encourages the child's right to develop a strong first language, to access the curriculum through his/her first language and to develop a strong identity and confidence as a deaf person. Inclusion involves more than just the school, it involves society too. Deaf people need to have the opportunity to develop languages and to access education, and hearing people need the opportunity to see deaf people as different not deficient.

This model of bilingual education in under-resourced schools has major implications in terms of planning and provision. It requires financial resources to provide appropriate training for teachers of the deaf and for enabling deaf people to train as teachers and instructors. It implies the placement of children in schools which may not be their local schools, with inevitable transport costs. In addition it implies the employment of a number of qualified staff to resource what is a small group of children in terms of the total number of children with special educational needs.

Issues of assessment in relation to the National Curriculum and public examinations need to be addressed. For instance, where all the testing is done on the basis of children having acquired their knowledge, skills and understanding in a particular framework and language, what changes have to be made so that the deaf children's real learning is assessed accurately? Proper study needs to be made into ascertaining the appropriate teaching methods involving developing a language based in one mode on the basis of a language learnt in another.

Additionally, inclusion must be seen as including families of deaf children and not just schools. Some deaf children will communicate better with their teachers than with their parents. Gregory's (1995) interviews with deaf adolescents indicate how many of them had limited communication at home or with other family members. A 19 year old BSL user explained, 'I talk to my mother, my father doesn't understand me'. A 22 year old who used BSL said (Gregory, 1995, p.41):

> My mother helps me understand my grandparents. I feel funny about her explaining because it's my own grandparents. I should be able to communicate with them directly.

It is important, therefore, that the needs of families are provided for. Pickersgill (1997) argues that pre-school services need to give sustained support to families and involve deaf people in this support. Opportunities to develop signing skills need to be available to parents and these need to be realistic opportunities, not just evening classes available at a location which may or may not be near the parents' home.

It could be argued that these support services need to be available beyond the pre-school stage as parents will need continuing help to develop their communication skills. At the same time, families with children who have a late diagnosis or who enter the country during their school career will also need support. A bilingual policy which enables the child to communicate well at school but leaves them isolated at home is not appropriate.

For the millennium there appear to be exciting possibilities and challenges in the development of bilingual education for deaf children.

A national policy of inclusive education needs to be interpreted broadly if bilingual policies as outlined above are to be implemented. Bilingualism may be an obstacle to the individual placement of deaf children in mainstream schools, However, it could enhance real opportunities for the linguistic growth of deaf children. In addition, the proper entitlement of these children to adequate educational opportunities and social and emotional development can be secured. A real understaning of the needs of these children will lead to commitment to policies that will support the children's inclusion, as part of a minority group, in the hearing world.

Bibliography

Baker, C. (1997), 'Deaf Children: Educating for Biligualism', in *Deafness and Education*, vol 21, no.3, pp. 3-9.

Baldwin, S. (1994), 'Full Inclusion: Reality versus Idealism', in *American Annals of the Deaf*, vol.139, no.2, pp. 164-165.

Bouvet, D. (1990), *The Path to Language: Bilingual Education for Deaf Children*, Multilingual Matters, Clevedon.

British Deaf Association (1996), *The Right to be Equal*, BDA, London.

Department for Education and Employment (1997), *Excellence for All*, Green Paper, DfEE, London.

Gallaway, C. and Woll, B. (1994), 'Interaction and Childhood Deafness', in Gallaway, C. and Richard, B., *Input and Interaction in Language Acquisition*, Cambridge University Press, Cambridge, UK.

Gregory, S. and Hartley, G. (eds) (1991), *Constructing Deafnes*, London; Pinter Press in association with the Open University, UK.

Gregory, S. (1995), *Deaf Young People and Their Families: Developing Understanding*, Cambridge University Press; Cambridge, UK.

Hall, J. (1997), *Social Devaluation and Special Education*, Jessica Kingsley, UK.

Harris, M. (1992*), Language Experience and Early Language Development*, Hove, Lawrence Erbaum Associates, USA.

Kirchner, A.0 (1994), 'Co-enrolment as an Inclusion Model', in *American Annals of the Deaf*, vol. 139, no. 2, pp.163-164.

Knight, P. (1997), 'Bilingual Nursery Provision: A Challenging Start', in *Deafness and Education*, vol. 21, no.3, pp. 20-30.

Kyle, J. and Woll, B. (1985), *Sign Language: The Study of Deaf People and Their Language*, Cambridge University Press, Cambridge, UK.

Ladd, P. (1991), 'The Modern Deaf Community', pp. 35-39 in Gregory, S. and Hartley, G., *Constructing Deafness*, Pinter Press in association with the Open University, London.

Lawson, L. (1991), 'The Role of Sign in the Structure of the Deaf Community', in Gregory, S. and Hartley, G., *Constructing Deafness*, Pinter Press in association with the Open University Press, London, pp. 31-34.

Marcshark, M. (1993, *Psychological Development of Deaf Children*, Oxford University Press, Oxford, UK.

Pickersgill, M. (1997), 'Towards a Model of Bilingual Education for Deaf Children', in *Deafness and Education*, vol.31, no. 3, pp. 10-19.

Powers, S. (1996) ,'Deaf Pupils' Achievements in Ordinary Schools', in *The Journal of the British Association of Teachers of the Deaf,* vol. 20, no. 3, pp. 111-123.

Stimson, M. and Lang, H. (1994), 'Full Inclusion: A Path for Integration or Isolation', in *American Annals of the Deaf,* vol. 139, no. 2, pp. 156-159.

12 Responding Locally to Global Inequality

PETER BLOOMFIELD

Abstract

The Earth Summit of world leaders in Rio de Janeiro in 1992 discussed environmental, social and sustainable development issues which should be the target, world wide, by the year 2000. The programme has become known as Agenda 21 and governments delegated much of the responsibility to local government, which led to the acronym, LA21. A catch-phrase summarises the aim, 'Think globally, act locally'. This chapter explores the global inequality of resources and resource consumption and the connection between being a local citizen and a global citizen. It argues that environmental equality affects people of all races, creeds and ethnicities.

It also highlights the significance of equality in a global context and the need for commitment within and outside the formal education sector for education for global justice to take place. Some local examples demonstrate possible limitations in knowledge about equality issues in the West. Meeting the challenges in the West can be done effectively only if education is interpreted as an exercise in collaboration amongst different individuals and organisations in any community. Real partnership between schools, community organisation, and a higher education institution is shown to be a key strategy for providing appropriately trained teachers.

Normally there is only limited interlinking between global development and issues of equality, another example of ghettoisation that has often led to the duplication of work and limited progress in any one area. Equality can feature in different contexts. A teaching approach that asks fundamental questions about equality and justice in relation to different people and countries and the world should have far reaching effects on developing sensitive, empathetic and committed adults and children as global as well as local citizens.

Introduction

At the outset of this chapter it is important to define Agenda 21 and to put it into context with similar world meetings. It is also necessary to investigate what is meant by 'equality' and to whom it applies. This may sound naive but far too often the 'everyone' answer is simply unrealistic and needs deconstructing temporally and spatially. However, if Agenda 21 really does relate to all peoples, everywhere, how will it achieve its goals? What are the implications for people being both local and global citizens? Agenda 21 as reported by Quarrie (1992) runs to several hundred pages of close print so this chapter explores small parts of the two strands of energy and food, provision and consumption. Developing the theme of interdependence, the roles of some of the world players, Indonesia, United States of America and United Kingdom are examined. Finally, a strategy is suggested for a way forward through education in the British system. Throughout this chapter the global, or macro, equality is related to local or personal equality.

What is Agenda 21 ?

World leaders, politicians, scientists, Non-Governmental Organisations (NGOs) such as UNICEF, Oxfam and Friends of the Earth and journalists met at a World Summit in Rio de Janeiro in 1992 to discuss the state of the planet and determine a way forward. Key issues discussed were resources, climate change, bio-diversity, pollution, and poverty. There were differences of opinion between the rich and the poor nations and between the rich nations, but the conference ended with 178 nation delegates signing agreements which proposed a way forward toward the twenty-first century. This document became known as Agenda 21. There are four main strands for action in Agenda 21:

- decreasing the use of raw materials and energy;
- reducing pollution and waste;
- protecting fragile environments;
- sharing wealth and responsibilities more fairly considering the needs of everyone.

Within the framework of Agenda 21 lies the concept of sustainability best defined as 'meeting the needs of the present without compromising the ability of future generations to meet their needs' (Bruntland, 1987). However, the difficulty of progression of Agenda 21 was recognised from the outset and governments delegated its implementation to local authorities within their countries, hence it became Local Agenda 21, or LA21. In Britain all local authorities (from county councils to district and parish councils) were charged with seeking a way forward and made accountable to central government. Action, for example, in reducing local traffic congestion and therefore pollution, in local and global contexts, was summarised in the catch phrase, 'Think globally, act locally'.

The Rio World Summit was followed by a progress summit in New York in July 1997. This was widely reported as a failure. One of the main issues facing the planet at the current time is that of climate change and its consequences for energy production and pollution. This was the subject of the Kyoto conference in Japan in December 1997.

How Equal is Equality in the Global Context?

From a fundamental moral standpoint it should be said that all people are equal. That being the case it is then difficult to quantify equality, if we wanted to. Could an uneducated peasant and a merchant banker exchange places? How would a graduate from the 'north' cope with daily life in the 'south'? Are all people equally resistant to all diseases? These very basic questions pose serious underlying problems and highlight the interdependence between people.

There are vast inequalities between people across the world in terms of wealth, literacy, nutrition, housing and education. If the world was a village of one hundred people, one would have university education, and seventy would be unable to read. The major problem confronting equity in the 21st century is that of starting with such inequality. The extremes between poor and rich, educated and uneducated, hungry and well fed are poles apart. The world's richest 30 per cent of people use 80 per cent of all the commercial energy (Quarrie, 1992). The poorest 70 per cent use only 20 per cent of all the energy. By extrapolation this means that the 30 per cent high energy consumers also use more primary resources in producing the majority of the energy; they may damage the environment to a greater extent in the extraction and refining processes, in transporting the raw material and then pollute the global atmosphere to a higher degree in the production of the energy. For instance, India has under 17 per cent of the world's population, and produces under 4 per cent of the world's carbon dioxide. The parallel figures for United States of America are 5 per cent and 25 per cent.

This pollution may lead to more global warming and more climate change. However, it is the poorest 70 per cent who suffer the most. They will take their toll from the global pollution and because they are poorer, may have less sturdy homes, have to build on inexpensive, marginal low lying land and may be less resistant to disease, and are often more prone to climatic hazards. These are the victims of hurricanes and floods in places such as Bangladesh, Mexico, China and the Philippines. The climatic change may also be effecting 'El Nino', the warming of the Pacific Ocean, which in turn seems to control monsoons, or lack of them, leading to drought, strong winds and hurricanes. The changing climate also seems to be responsible for the reduced snow fall on the mountains of Columbia. Here the Kogi people, an ancient isolated South American rainforest tribe who consider themselves as 'elder brothers' of the world, have accused the developed world ('younger brothers') of 'stealing the snow'. The once snow capped mountains are often bare, meltwater is greatly reduced, as is water in the rivers, the Kogi's source of life.

The other example to illustrate the inequalities is food. During World War Two the biggest non-military threat to Britain, as an island, was starvation. Britain was not self sufficient and dreaded the consequences of imports being severed. As a result post-war agricultural policy has been to aim for self sufficiency at all costs. During the war this was promoted by 'Dig for Victory' and later through many government incentives promoting greater technology, (machines and chemicals) larger farms, fields and herds, subsidies and grants. When the UK joined the European Economic Community (then European Community and now European Union) where similar advances were being made, guaranteed prices were paid for agricultural produce. This eventually led to over-production of some commodities and in the 1980s, mountains of grain and butter, lakes of milk and freezers full of beef were building up over Britain and Europe. Quotas were imposed to stem the over- production.

Despite this, Britain currently imports between 40 per cent and 50 per cent of its food! British tastes have diversified and food is imported from all over the world. For instance, Britain buys palm oil products, pineapples and others from Indonesia. In April 1997 countless fires were started in Indonesia to clear virgin rainforest and old plantations to make space to plant new crops. This traditional method of clearing small plots of land is now used for larger areas, often illegally, the fires usually being extinguished by seasonal monsoons before cultivation takes place. In 1997 the monsoons had not arrived even by November and all that Indonesia exported was smoke and smog pollution for up to 1000 miles. In holiday resorts tourists were choking, and thousands of people across South-east Asia needed medical help for respiratory infections. There are dilemmas. Citizens of the rich North have grown to expect cheap products from the poor citizens in the South. Rainforst dwellers are told by the North *not* to cut or burn their trees. However, they can justifiably turn around and say that they needed the money for food and education, fridges and television sets.

Local Citizens being Good Global Citizens

For many of the 'rich' in the world giving to charity is seen as being a global citizen. In the North millions of pounds are given in aid to projects in Third World, for example, the use of intermediate technology energy saving stoves. This giving is highly commendable and should be supported. It is thinking and acting as a global citizen, but it is only the tip of the iceberg in being an effective global citizen. What is involved in acting locally? Should we not reduce *our* energy consumption and pollution? Taking the example of the USA, 5 per cent of the world population creates 20 per cent of the world pollution. In 1997 USA donated one billion dollars to the Tthird World to reduce Third World pollution. The USA claimed that by supporting non-polluting development in the Third World they are reducing global pollution. However, in their own country emission restraints or targets are almost non-existent. This is not acting locally, and is just another example of the NIMBY (Not in My Back Yard) phenomenon which illustrates how the wealthy can attempt to buy their way out of making a commitment to environmental equity. The Indonesian smogs have claimed many lives far away from the source of the pollution. So it is very clear why the USA (and Europe) should do all they can to reduce their pollution before it affects many others in the global village. Being equal means that local energy consumption has to be lowered to reduce lower carbon dioxide emissions. The United Kingdom needs to address many environmental pressures (Selman, 1996):

- population growth;
- global atmosphere;
- air quality;
- freshwater;
- sea;
- soil;
- land use;
- minerals;
- wildlife and habitats;
- transport;
- energy;
- waste.

Opportunities for acting locally are funded in the context of these problems (Selman, 1996):

- in regional population pressure areas, (migration to SE England);
- reducing carbon-dioxide, and greenhouse gasses;

- vehicle pollution (this is a serious problem);
- freshwater conservation, pollution from agri-chemicals;
- estuarine pollution and depletion of fish stocks;
- contaminated soil and other land;
- demands for roads and housing on 'sensitive' land;
- loss of biodiversity and habitats on 'temperate' island location;
- serious transport problems; congestion, air pollution, noise;
- energy efficiency and waste management (including nuclear);
- waste / package management; need to reuse, recycle and recover.

There are many ways in which local action can be implemented with resulting global benefits. Some of this action may be local authority led, or NGO led but much can be achieved by the individual. One further strand should be considered in striving for equity and sustainability, the role of education. Schumacher (1973) believes that 'Education is the greatest resource'.

The Role of Education

Sustainability has often been interpreted as looking after the planet for our children, as the earth is borrowed from our children. Future generations are thus at the heart of Agenda 21 and sustainability; and they need to be educated as global citizens. For Wade (1997, p.11):

> This brings us back to the key questions: what kind of society and world do we want for our grandchildren? What are the values needed to ensure that there are enough resources left for the coming generations while also addressing the needs of millions who are living in poverty *now*?

The Rt Hon, Gillian Shephard MP, then Secretary of State for Education and Employment, went part way to answering these questions in a speech to the Education and Environment Conference (SCAA, 1996) by stating that 'as the citizens of tomorrow, the pupils of today' will be involved in framing national decisions about the allocation of resources with profound consequences for the environment. They would need to understand what is meant by 'global warming' or 'biodiversity' or 'sustainable development', and how great or how small are the risks of environmental damage associated with different policies.

Others have made strong representations to include the concepts of Agenda 21 in the curriculum. Thirty years before Mrs Shephard's speech, an educational report saw a school merely as a teaching shop, but all with transmitted values and attitudes. Education should enable children to become balanced and mature adults, being able to live in, contribute, and look critically at their society (Plowden, 1967).

In this decade commentators have been more specific. Lovelock (1991) believes we need ' a new profession, (of teachers) concerned with the health of the planet and practising planetary preventive medicine'. Orr (1993, p.16) agrees:

> Students of the next century will need to know how to create a civilisation that runs onsunlight, conserves energy, preserves biodiversity, protects soils and forests, develops sustainable local economies and restores the damage inflicted on the Earth. In order to achieve such ecological education we need to transform our schools and universities

However, it is not sufficient simply to change, for example, infant education in the hope that future generations will become more aware and steer toward a sustainable and equitable world. There is a need for partnership nd continuity throughout all stages of education and in communities where the institutes are located.

Partnership Education Through LA21 in Hertfordshire

A recent small scale research project in Hertfordshire uncovered a great lack of awareness of LA21 in primary schools (Bloomfield, 1997). However, that is not to say that these schools are lacking in knowledge about environmental issues. Far from it, most have built environmental studies into their curriculum through science or geography or Personal, Health, and Social Education courses. However this rarely involves full Agenda 21 participation.

The Department of Education at the University of Hertfordshire has developed an optional course for students who are training to be primary school teachers, 'Environmental Education: Global Perspectives in the 21st Century', in the third and fourth year of their BEd degree. University tutors are working with headteachers and staff in local primary schools, the local authority, local LA21 Forum (60 organisations including business, NGOs, water company, schools, and church groups), and the local MP to develop the new course. The concept is that the university, students, schools, local authority and community work in partnership on LA21 projects. These projects will be cross curricular, involve the local community and address the concept of sustainability (Figure12.1). University Partnership School staff are encouraged to attend and participate in lectures and workshops and expect to have a total of 36 student hours in their school to develop a negotiated LA21 project which will be run by the students, completed or left viable to be confirmed by the class teachers. University tutors, school staff and students are being encouraged to develop environmental and citizenship style courses across as many National Curriculum subjects as possible to support a community based project. However, it will be the responsibility of the University students to translate the project into activities across the National Curriculum. Special attention will be given to literacy, numeracy and Information Technology in planning and implementing the work with the children. The Key Stages 1 and 2 themes in Geography, 'Local Area', 'Contrasting Locality' and 'Environment' underpin the school work.

The ideal model of schools nominating community based projects has encountered several stumbling blocks, concerned not least with security and safety fears. Hillman (1998) gives some of the reasons. The local neighbourhood used to provide a unique place for children to develop basic physical, social and geographical skills without adult supervision. However, parental fears about the dangers of traffic and possible molestation by strangers has led to growing restrictions being placed on children's freedom. This fear and the post Dunblane security reinforcements have led partnership schools to restrict their suggestions to those which occupy the school grounds and minimise contact with the community. Examples of the proposed projects are:

- conversion of 'outside rooms' into bird hides along with planting of bird attracting plants;
- developing two environmental trails, one in the school grounds and an extension in adjacent Park, the latter to be open to the public;
- developing an outdoor classroom (literally) and making use of the adjacent river;
- Completion of already existing plans for an exploratory environmental trrail around the school grounds, in conjunction with the parish council and parents;
- development of quiet areas away from the football grounds;
- creating a sculpture trail and willow tunnel.

If the children identify with and are taught that their actions are helping in the local environment, and that this could have global significance, no matter how small, then LA21 will be seen to be alive and well. The students will evaluate the projects through an assignment and that assessment will contribute toward their degree. They will have learnt how to include interesting, meaningful, real world activities into their teaching.

Figure 12.1 An Example of LA 21

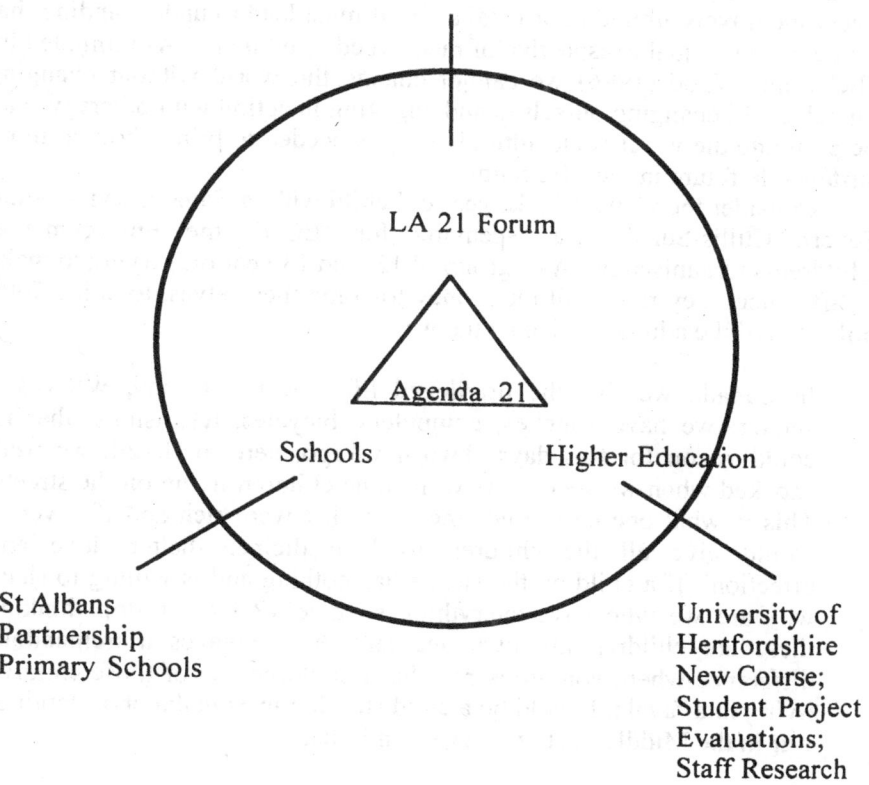

Does Agenda 21 mean Equality in the 21st century?

The answer to this question is that it is not necessarily the case. There are many obstacles. For instance Shah (1996) suggests that focuses such as global education are still likely to be categorised as left wing radical politics, as opposed to 'good' education. However, progress can be made if initiatives are taken at home, the workplace, the school and in the way everyone travels around their local area.. It must lead to understanding that all people are equal irrespective of race, creed or ethnicity. As reminded by Hicks and Wood (1996) we cannot change the world without changing ourselves. In changing ourselves and engaging in action with others we can help initiate the wider sociocultural changes needed to bring about a more sustainable future in the 21st century.

Consider the views of a 12 year old child with a Canadian viewpoint. Severn Cullis-Suzuki was speaking for 'ECO', the Environmental Children's Organisation. As a group of 12 and 13 year olds trying to make a difference, they raised all the money to come themselves, to come 5000 miles to tell the adults to change the ways:

> In Canada we live the privileged life. Plenty of food, water and shelter; we have watches, computers, bicycles, televisions...the list could go on for two days. Two days ago, here in Brazil, we were shocked when we spent time with some children living on the streets. This is what one child told me, 'I wish I were rich and if I were I would give all the children food, medicine, shelter, love and affection'. If a child on the streets has nothing and is willing to share why are we who have everything so greedy? I can't stop thinking these are children my own age and that it makes a tremendous difference where you are born. That I could be one of those children living in a favala; I could be a child starving in Somalia or a victim of war in the Middle East or a beggar in India.

The speech was made to Rio World Summit in 1992. A video copy of the speech was presented to World Education Felloship International Conference in Kuching, Sarawak, Malaysia in August 1996. The speech is quoted here by kind permission of Severn Cullis-Suzuki.

Severn identifies equality of resources and resource consumption (North/South); clean air, drinking water, land, food, energy and biodiversity. She tries to put herself in other contexts, in other people's shoes. As a minority world citizen she will live most of her life in the 21st century. What Severn said may have been from a child, but gets to the very heart of the link between Agenda 21 and equity between people.

Bibliography

Bloomfield, P. (1998), 'Raising Awareness of Local Agenda 21', in Scoffham, S. (ed), *Primary Sources, Research Findings in Primary Geography*, pp. 34-35, Geography Association, Sheffield, UK.

Brown, P. (1997), 'Global Warming: The Planet's Hottest Problem', in *The Guardian*, October 10.

Bruntland, G. (1987), *Our Common Future* (The Bruntland Report), World Commission on Environment and Development (WCED), Oxford University Press, Oxford, UK.

Hicks, D. and Wood, K. (1996), 'Re-enchanting the World: Education for Change in the 1990s', in Steiner, M. (ed), *Developing the Global Teacher*, pp. 103-110, Trentham Books, Stoke-on-Trent, UK.

Hillman, M. (1998), 'Neighbourhood Safety', in Scoffham, S. (ed) *Primary Sources, Research Findings in Primary Geography*, pp. 28-29, Geography Association, Sheffield, UK.

Lovelock, J.E. (1991), 'Planetary Medicine', in *Resurgence*, Issue 148, pp. 37-8.

Meadows, D. (1997) 'Not so Fast, in *Resurgence*, Issue 184.

National Curriculum Council (1990), *Curriculum Guidance Booklet 7, Environmental Education*, York, UK.

National Curriculum Council (1990), *Curriculum Guidance Booklet 8, Education for Citizenship*, York, UK.

Orr, D. (1993), 'Schools for the Twenty-first Century', in *Resurgence*, Issue 160, p.117.

Plowden, B. (1967), *Children and their Primary Schools*, HMSO, London.

Quarrie, J. (1992), *Earth Summit 1992*, The Regency Press, London, UK.

Schools Curriculum and Assessment Authority (1996), *Teaching Environmental Matters through the National Curriculum*, SCAA, London.

Schumacher, E. F. (1973), *Small is Beautiful*, Abacus, London.

Selman, P. (1996), *Local Sustainability*, Paul Chapman Publishing, London.

Shah, S. (1996), 'Inital Teacher Education and Global Citizenship: the Context of Permeation', in Steiner, M. (ed), *Developing the Global Teacher*, pp. 55-62, Trentham Books, Stoke-on-Trent, UK.

Wade, R. (1997), 'Educationg for the 21st Century', in Inman, S. and Wade, R., *Shaping a Better Future*, pp. 1-26, Oxfam, UK.

13 Democracy and Education

SÉAN STITT

Abstract

The aim of this chapter is to expose a paradox permeating teaching. Educational professionals, in general, perceive teaching as, what is euphemistically known, a 'caring profession' and a preparatory system for living in a democracy. However, no substantive developments towards the 'democratisation' of education have occurred. The outcome is that, while children are legally compelled to attend school, their democratic rights and freedoms are greatly endangered and uncatered for at school. Children who are different because of their class, race, religion, ability, sexuality etc. are more vulnerable to damage by the education system manifesting in higher non-completion rates, low attainment standards, fewer opportunities at higher education level and, indeed, abuse.

The chapter also considers the role of some human rights legislation which forces educational professionals into 'democratising' education, by challenging the understanding of the qualities of a 'good educator' and the training and selection of educational professionals. It examines developments required within education to synchronise it with human rights charters' demands for democratic education.

It is necessary to accept that focusing on specific aspects of equality in the new millennium can be 'only tinkering' with the system. Equality can be attained in a system that provides education results from a serious and comprehensive analysis of the links of education with society.

Introduction

There is a paradox permeating teaching. Educational professionals, in general, perceive teaching as, what is euphemistically known to be, a 'caring profession' and a preparatory system for living in a democracy. However, there have been no significant developments towards the 'democratisation' of education. The key obstacle to this process of 'democratisation' continues to be the nervous reluctance of the educational system supported by traditional school governance and educational professionals. With regard to the educational status quo, it is agnostic about human rights issues, problems and the various documents and charters which address these areas; it is unaware of the legal system's interpretation of human right declarations; and finally, it is uninterested in the ethical considerations influencing the interaction between children/students and their human rights environment.

The outcome is that while children are legally compelled to attend school, their democratic rights and freedoms are greatly endangered and uncatered for at school. The main reason is well put by Major (1993, p.144):

> Discipline and self respect ... Let us return to basic subject teaching, not courses in the theory of education. Primary teachers should... not waste their time on the politics of race, class and gender. Children who are 'different' because of their class, race, religion, ability, sexuality etc. are more vulnerable to damage by the education system, manifesting in higher non-completion rates, low attainment standards, fewer opportunities at higher education level and, indeed, abuse.

Mullard (1980) sees education as a meaningless process. It is only worthwhile if it is concerned with the struggle against the different forms of tyranny, caused by ignorance, oppression, inequality or exploitation.

The Need for Human Rights Education

Human rights are ours by nature of being human and are ours from birth. Logically - but unfortunately not in practice- human rights also apply in schools. Respect for one another, full entitlement to the curriculum, policies to ensure equality for all members of the school community, conscious and sustained efforts to make the school environment a place where rights and responsibilities are respected and encouraged, are all example of rights in action in schools. An understanding of the content of the most important of these international human rights statements, the Universal Declaration of Human Rights, and how it affects the daily life of primary schools is the subject of this chapter. The Council of Europe is convinced that education can make a vital contribution to the promotion and protection of human rights. It recommends that there should be a common core to human rights education, consisting of (Stobart in Starkey, 1991):

- the main categories of human rights, duties, obligations and responsibilities;
- the various forms of injustice, inequality and discrimination, including elitism, racism and sexism;
- people, movements and key events in the historic and continuing struggle for human rights;
- the main international declarations and conventions on human rights - e.g., the Universal Declaration of Human Rights and the European Convention for the Protection of Human Rights and Fundamental Freedoms.

Among the skills needed for understanding and supporting human rights, the Council of Europe attaches special importance to the following (Starkey, 1991):

- skills associated with language development, such as written and oral expression and the ability to discuss and listen;
- skills involving judgements- the collection and analysis of material from various sources (including the mass media); the detection of bias, prejudice and stereotypes; and the ability to arrive at fair and balanced conclusions;
- social skills, including the recognition and acceptance of differences and the ability to establish positive and non-oppressive personal relationships;
- action skills such as participating in group decisions, solving conflict in a non-violent way, taking responsibility, and using the mechanisms for the protection of human rights that exist at local, national, European and global levels.

Thus human rights education helps pupils to develop a repertoire of skills and concepts which make up a mental tool box. Pupils can carry this 'box' from one context to another and draw upon it to construct frameworks for understanding human rights issues in their different forms. An instructional unit about South African apartheid should, for example, challenge the students to acquire much more than just knowledge about it. The activities should develop pupil understanding of pluralism, institutional racism and violence, distribution of power and resources, class system, self-determination and international law, all of which can be applied to situations beyond South Africa (the North of Ireland, the Middle East). The unit should also challenge pupils to come to terms with conflicting conceptions of freedom, justice and equality, slavery, civil rights, sexism, globalism etc. (Kohler, 1978).

Further, in the process of seeking to achieve this, human rights education must not only reject all forms of authoritarianism but it must:

> also assist pupils in the process of protecting themselves against other forces and agencies within society 'which would seek to do their thinking for them' (Kelly, 1995). This is part of that function of education which was Paulo Freire's (1972) sole justification for its provision, the function of 'alarming' young people against all those agencies which seek to ensure that they are 'dopes' whose destinies can be planned for them.

Obstacles to Human Rights Education

There are many agencies in society which have a vested interest in discouraging autonomous thinking and reflection and not only in the young. Politicians, for example, want people to accept their policies without too much detailed analysis. And manufacturers want everyone to purchase their products without too much careful inspection or comparison with alternatives. This is the point and purpose of advertising, whether commercial or political. In neither case is it aimed at encouraging challenge, critique, debate or reflection. On the contrary, it is concerned to discourage that kind of approach and to promote a largely uncritical acceptance of its offerings. Human rights education is opposed even by specific focus/pressure groups because it involves issues beyond their narrow, myopic view of the denial of rights to their interest group. Criticisms of human rights education, have included points such as:

- it is a waste of time; the real need is for the challenging of the structure which does not give the children their basic rights;
- it allows teachers to fudge the issues of racism and sexism;
- children may become convinced that they would also be actively involved which is not relevant to children and their education;
- children do not talk as much about the responsibility as about their rights.

Within the context of human rights, such uncritical acceptance must be rejected. And so, human rights education must seek positively to counteract complacency. It must set about this by encouraging that critical, inquiring, challenging approach which is essential to all forms of education in a democratic society. It must also however take a more positive stance than this. It must offer pupils opportunities to look critically at aspects of current society and help them to develop those critical faculties which they need if they are to learn to see beyond rhetoric or to avoid forfeiting their own human rights and the manipulation of their thinking by agencies in society which are concerned only to promote their own sectional interests.

Morality and Teaching

Even where there are enforcement mechanisms and courts, as with the European Convention on Human Rights, education is still indispensable. Legal force of itself is only a secondary safety valve; it is the education of young people and adults, according to Rene Cassin, Nobel Peace Prize winner 1968 (Starkey 1991) that constitutes the primary and real guarantee for minority groups faced with racial hatred that leads so easily to violence and murder.

Two conservative spokespersons referring to the 'purpose of law', 'moral responsibility', 'taking responsibility for one's actions', implied that incorporating human rights education into primary schools equates with discovering or re-discovering an individual moral education approach to the agenda. The examples are taken from Rowe and Newton (1994). Secretary of State for the Home Office, Michael Howard MP stated that a society needs responsible citizens capable of understanding the purpose of law and respecting the rights of others. The then Secretary of State for Education, Gillian Shephard MP, saw a specific role of education for citizenship when she stated that the development of positive attitudes towards citizenship, which was the taking of responsibility for one's actions, and having respect for others, were a cornerstone of a civilised society. These values could not be instilled early enough.

Abdallah-Retceille (1991) elaborated on this, seeing education as inculcating references classified by degrees of good and evil which lead to human rights becoming the yardstick by which all other systems of values are measured. This approach involves the school in the transmission of a moral code, that of human rights. But a clear contradiction is apparent in this reduction of the universality of human rights to a specific moral code which, by logic, is likely to be rejected in the very name of the right to be different. Human rights education would be conceived of as the transmission of model attitudes and values and would be reliant on a certain form of compulsion. This, is highly prescriptive, which goes hand-in glove with a particular form of moral/religious education, but is clearly the antithesis of human rights education which focuses on the rejection of any form of coercion/regulation/standardisation. The reality is that human rights education simply cannot be diminished down to any theme of a moral code, even of a secular nature.

Children and Perceptions of Human Rights

Human rights are at the core of children's everyday life experiences- freedom of thought, conscience, religion (and freedom from religion), values, morality, the right to education- and the essence of education is to empower children to make sense of the world around them. Many also confront a denial/infringement of their rights through bullying, name-calling, abuse etc. Being aware of rights and responsibilities, understanding the struggles which have been sacrificed to achieve these are all vital components in the preparation of all young citizens living in (theoretically) a democratic and pluralist society. When a child protests 'That's not fair', s/he is demonstrating awareness of human rights, justice and equality. Consider the following poem by a five year old school child (Steiner, 1993, p.4):

> The teachers all sit in the classroom
> The teachers all drink, tea,
> The teachers all smoke cigarettes
> As cosy as can be.
> We have to play out at playtime
> Unless we bring a note,
> Or it's tipping down with rain or
> We have not got a coat.
> We have to go out at playtime
> Whether we like it or not,
> And freeze to death if it's freezing,
> And boil to death if it's hot.
> The teachers can sit in the staffroom,
> And have a cosy chat.
> We have to go out at playtime,
> *Where's the fairness in that?*

Human rights education should reinforce this innate sense of justice/injustice, the need for 'fair play' and explore the casual factors behind unfairness (Miller and Miller, 1990).

Values and the Hidden Curriculum

For many pupils, parents and teachers, state schools do not seem to embrace any shared value system. Where there are shared values, they tend to focus on what should not occur and such value systems confer neither rights nor responsibilities. In the experience of Lyseith-Jones (1991), Inspector for Primary Education for the London Borough of Ealing, the criteria by which decisions are made are 'secret' and 'probably flexible'. She has confronted such situations in which the decision-maker and values-creator has much scope for manipulation, whether benign or not. A focal role for the human rights educator is thus to help a school to define the values which it shares, the unbreakable tents of that value system, the negotiable elements of it, the operationalizing of it and the publicity which should surround its development, implementation and revision. Elsewhere, Lyseight-Jones (1985) argues that the human rights teacher should try to examine what children may be learning from the hidden curriculum. Pupils are asked to pick up on non-verbal messages from each other. The following exemplify what she means by this:

- talking only permitted when sanctioned by their teacher;
- children having to seek permission to use the toilets;
- irrelevant, unjust and unfair sanctions;
- the use of grading systems whose main purpose is the identification of an elite and which 'promotes the few at the expense of many children's family patterns not being respected by the teacher;
- the teacher making little or not effort to have in the classroom items and information which are familiar to the children and their backgrounds;
- decisions being made by the teacher alone;
- the teacher unable to perceive the place and role of humour and levity in the classroom.

Such facets of the hidden curriculum may serve to expose fine words, just a ruse to cover up the lack of commitment to the principles of human rights education.

Policy Intervention

Before current policies and practices, and in particular the National Curriculum in Britain are evaluated, it is important to recognise that in many ways, these have gone against the stream of educational developments taking us towards the reconceptualization which democratic principles demand. They have done so to such an extent that they can only be regarded as a deliberate attempt to halt the flow of that stream, not only to prevent any response from the education system to postmodernism but also to hold up the democratisation of education and social provision in general. Thus the National Curriculum makes it even more important that human rights education is woven into the system as a counter balance to the basic, instrumental, 'value-for-money' ideology of that curriculum and particularly necessary in the context of a curriculum which is framed in terms of subjects rather than 'areas of experience', and where those subjects are conceived in terms of 'useful knowledge to be acquired rather than in terms of the contribution they make to the overall development of the individual and human rights. As Kelly (1995, p.176) asserts:

> The National Curriculum is conceived and planned simply as a vehicle for the acquisition of knowledge and not as a support for (human rights) through that acquisition. And so it can no more support (human rights education) that it can promote any other kind of development.

It is for this reason that the National Curriculum (National Curriculum Council, 1990) has identified as a 'cross-curricular' theme, personal and social education. However, anything which is not specified and prescribed and which thus does not contribute to 'league table points' is inevitably regarded as of lesser importance and thus marginalized, so that personal and social education becomes a kind of optional extra rather than being accepted as none of the most important tasks of the schools. There is no logic in a government imposing policies that marginalize personal, social and moral education and then castigating parents and teachers for an apparent decline in behavioural standards and tolerance among the young. The change in terminology from 'moral' to 'personal and social' may denote that the approach to this area of the curriculum is inadequate and inappropriate when evaluated against the criteria for human rights education in a democratic society. There is more of a flavour of question for conformity about it than of education for autonomy.

The concern which motivates research that is described below was that after 18 years of the Conservative government's interference in, manipulation of, and dictating to, the education system on what should be taught and how it should be taught, culminating in the National Curriculum, values/morals/social/rights education would have evolved along with a Right-wing perspective on human rights. Some informed critical reactions to the National Curriculum attempt to relate its structure and content directly to the general political philosophy of the government of the day. Ahier and Ross (1995, p.3) argue that:

> This suspicion is that 'the social' would somehow cease to be a focus for education. Given the public denials of the very existence of society by Margaret Thatcher, and the belief held by her, and other followers of Hayeck, that society cannot be 'made' by political initiatives (or what they call state interference), then it is argued that the new curriculum is, in essence, more about individual competition and instrumental achievement than it is about (human rights).

The move away from human rights and other social studies since the 1988 Education Reform Act is strangely out of kilter with international trends. In so may of the countries that are currently cast in the role of Britain's economic competitors, human rights education has assumed an increasing proportion of curricular time. But in Britain, the description and practice of this element of studies has gone into decline. Although the cross-curricular themes which emerged may be seen as reintroducing 'the social' in the curriculum, it has been a very different ideal of 'the social' to that which had been developed and jettisoned in the last two decades. For example, in the area of health education, there is more stress on the duty of the individual to 'behave responsibly', to take evasive action, to plan their lifestyle, diet, fitness regime etc., in such a way that minimises their future call on state-provided services. The emphasis is to stress the role of the individual, rather than any corporate roles, duties, responsibilities and obligations (of the individual to the state) are placed before any human rights or expectations the individual might have of the state. The primary target of radical Right wrath has been, and remains, the Leftist elements with their anti-elitism, stress on democratic human rights education by overtly critiquing and confronting exploitation, racism, sexism, homophobia and social class inequalities in schooling, as well as in society- the 'Blue Peter Curriculum' (Cole, Hill and Shan, 1997).

The last decade has witnessed many major alterations in the concepts and practice of a comprehensive, holistic education. The national policy objectives of the early 1980s focused on theoretical concern for social justice. But the beginning of the 1990s, these had been overtaken by the momentum to increase education productivity, via a return to the free market place and by a diminution of promotion of human rights education. The Department of Education and Science (DES) blueprint for the National Curriculum, hastily devised in 1987, is thus subject-based. Any area of educational experience which falls outside its subject framework has generally faced neglect, like multiculturalism, and egalitarian education. The National Curriculum driven more by the theme of cultural homogeneity than by the promotion of human rights. It became an embodiment of a Conservative vision of a national culture. Besides being subject-based, it is also content led - i.e. issues connected with the learning process are not adequately explored. According to Cole et al (1997) one of the several debilitating consequences of this approach is that issues which have implications for the ways in which different groups of pupils related to the formal, organised knowledge of the school are not explored. Human rights issues, whether related to class, race, gender, disability, special needs or sexuality have not been prominent. The result is not simply that particular areas of content are incomplete, but that quite basic issues concerning the relationship between curriculum and learner, formal education and pupil cultures, have generally been left unexplored. The 1995 Dearing revisions of the National Curriculum ('slimming down', five-year moratorium on changes etc.) do not answer the criticisms outlined in this chapter. The Dearing recommendations have created problems of their own; as detailed by King and Mitchell (1995, p.20):

> that is, unless schools and teachers can be persuaded to use these promised reductions in the compulsory curriculum to pursue (human rights education) and multicultural and antiracist goals. Significantly, the final Dearing Report makes no mention on multicultural (or human rights) education at all.

Education in human rights will not develop unless teachers are first of all convinced of the need to teach human rights, then given special training in the methods of such teaching. This task falls largely on the shoulders of universities and colleges providing teacher training courses.

Research Project

Thus research was undertaken to investigate the nature and extent of concern among (primary) teacher training undergraduates and PGCE students at John Moores University Liverpool (LJMU), the biggest teacher training centre in the North West of England. It also sought to establish the professional interest in reinforcing existing rights education and expanding it to cover more contemporary phenomenon-like refugees, the European Union, growing women's equality and growing men's inequality, Third World exploitation, the 'underclass', and so on.

A survey was carried out among a sample of 100 students at LJMU. The essential/core findings of the survey showed that, of those who expressed an opinion, 87 per cent believed that human rights education in primary schools currently was 'inadequate', 72 per cent believed that the government of the day can and does influence human rights education. Yet 90 per cent could not explain the implications of the Universal Declaration of Human Rights for primary school teaching, and 47 per cent had never heard of this convention.

When asked about formation of policies, 80 per cent expressed 'little' or 'no' confidence in a Labour government improving and radicalising' human rights education. In the opinion of 65 per cent, civil servants should not be involved in constructing a human rights curriculum (many anecdotally stating that they were not 'impartial' or 'independent'). A large number, 85 per cent, believed that such a curriculum should be influenced more by the teaching profession, parents and children than by the government of the day. Then a number of assertions were put to the sample. The students were asked to strongly agree through to strongly disagree. The results of this exercise are set out in Table 13.1. The assertions were as follows:

(1) There has been a re-emergence of public expression of racism and xenophobia.
(2) Many young people are becoming increasingly affected by economic recession, growing poverty and inequality.
(3) Primary school education reaffirms democratic values in the face of intolerance, violence and terrorism (including state terrorism).
(4) All young people should learn about human rights as part of their preparation for life in a pluralistic democracy.
(5) Primary schools are communities which can, and should, be an example of respect for the dignity of the individual and for difference, for tolerance and for equality of opportunity.

(6) The emphasis in teaching and learning about human rights should be positive. Pupils may be led by feelings of powerlessness and discouragement when confronted with many examples of violations and negation of human rights. Instances of progress and success should be used.

(7) The study of human rights in schools should lead to an understanding of, and sympathy for, the concepts of justice, equality, freedom, peace, dignity, rights and democracy. Such understanding should be both cognitive and based on experience and feelings. Schools should thus provide opportunities for pupils to experience affective involvement in human rights and to express their feelings through drama, art, music, creative writing and audio-visual media.

(8) Initial training of teachers prepares them for their future contribution to teaching about human rights in their schools.

(9) Teacher training encourages an interest in national and world affairs.

(10) Teacher training provides the opportunity to study/work in a foreign country or in a different environment.

(11) Teacher training familiarises with the main international declarations and conventions on human rights.

(12) Teacher training familiarises with the workings and achievements of the international organisations which deal with the protection and promotion of human rights, for example through visits and study tours.

(13) All teachers need, and should be given the opportunity to update their knowledge and to learn new methods through in-service training, including the study of good practice and teaching about human rights, as well as the development of appropriate methods and materials.

(14) Teaching human rights is a waste of time. Instead what we really need to be doing is challenging the structure in schools which deny pupils their basic rights.

(15) Thinking in terms of human rights education is an easy way out- it allows teachers to fudge the issues and avoid taking a strong antiracist and antisexist stance.

(16) If children learn about human rights and campaigns, they may want to get involved in campaigns. It is not the role of teachers and schools to become involved in such campaigns.

(17) Children are encouraged to think too much about rights and not enough about their responsibilities.

(18) Schools and teacher training establishments should be encouraged to observe International Human Rights Day (December 10th).

154 *Equality Issues for the New Millennium*

Other days mentioned, by some only, were Martin Luther King (January 15th); International Women's (March 8th); World Health (April 7th); International Children's (June 1st); World Environment (June 5th); Hiroshima (August 6th); United Nations (October 24th). When asked about the focus of human rights education, the main themes to emerge were:

- peace studies;
- women's rights;
- men's rights;
- celebration of cultural diversity in schools; and teacher training colleges;
- ethnic minority rights;
- gay and lesbian rights;
- rights of the disabled;
- racial equality;
- secular rights (the right to be atheist/agnostic);
- humanist rights (the right to be atheist/agnostic);
- liberation struggles throughout the world;
- solidarity;
- the Third World;
- environmental/animal rights.

Conclusion

According to Lyseight-Jones (1991), where there are conflicting rights, the duty of the primary school teacher is to protect the most vulnerable and least powerful. There is clearly the need for the establishment of a working body of teachers, educationalists, parents and pupils groups to proceed on a new and radical programme for comprehensive human rights education for all pupils, centred on class, race, ability, secularity, religion and atheism, gender and other themes, and the reversal of the Christian-centred emphasis which has dictated such education since the mid-1970s. This would necessarily involve a rejection of a prescriptive approach by dictating moral codes to pupils and the acceptance of an education and socialisation based on interpersonal relations and exchanges between the individual and his/her environment. The practicalities of this concept are clarified by Abdallah-Pretceille (1991, p.64):

> Placed at the centre of the educational process, the child is elevated to the status of actor and subject.

Table 13.1 Student teachers' views on human rights education

Assertion No	Strongly Agree %	Agree %	Don't Know %	Disagree %	Strongly Disagree %
(1)	55	35	0	7	3
(2)	43	29	8	16	4
(3)	12	17	21	27	23
(4)	82	8	1	8	1
(5)	66	19	6	5	4
(6)	78	12	2	4	4
(7)	29	44	5	12	10
(8)	12	22	15	36	15
(9)	18	17	5	42	18
(10)	7	7	2	71	13
(11)	14	27	15	35	9
(12)	4	7	5	69	15
(13)	61	24	3	7	5
(14)	12	14	20	38	8
(15)	10	13	38	20	19
(16)	12	4	4	68	12
(17)	18	28	5	30	21
(18)	69	19	8	4	0

He goes on to say that (Abdallah-Pretceille, 1991, p.64):

> confronted on one hand by the adult a person riddled with contradictions, and on the other hand by his/her cultural background also charged with meanings and marked by values which may indeed be contradictory, now and then ...

So contextualized, human rights education is no longer a matter of diktats, orders or imposed standards, but an exercise in the evolution of educational and pedagogic dynamics. Thus human rights education cannot simply be added to the curriculum of schools as another subject. It is characterised by an identifiable educational ideology concerned with helping individuals to become active participants in their own development, rather than passive recipients of educational diktats.

Human rights education has been conceptualised in terms of an education in moral literacy', and perhaps even an education in civil courage. Societies throughout the world need both of these approaches if each is capable of eliminating the intolerance, prejudice and conflict created by poverty, unemployment and inequality.

Bibliography

Abdallah-Pretceille, A. (1991), 'Human Rights in the Nursery School', in Starkey, H., *The Challenge of Human Rights Education*, Cassell, London.
Ahier, J. and Ross, A. (1995), *The Social Subjects Within the Curriculum*, Falmer Press, London.
Freire, P. (1972), *Pedagogy of the Oppressed*, Penguin Books, London.
Cole, M., Hill, D. and Shan, S. (1997), *Promoting Equality in Primary Schools*, Cassell, London.
Kelly, A.V. (1995), *Education and Democracy: Principles and Practices*, Paul Chapman Publishing, London.
King, A. and Mitchell, P. (1995), 'The National Curriculum and Ethnic Relations', in Tomlinson, S. and Craft, M. (eds), *Ethnic Relations and Schooling*, Athlone Press, London.
Kohler, G. (1978), *Global Apartheid*, Centre for International Studies, Princeton University, USA.
Lyseight-Jones, P. (1985), *Council of Europe Teacher Seminar on Human Rights in Primary Schools*, Council of Europe, DECS/EGT(85) 46-E, Council of Europe, Strasbourg.
Major, J. (1993), Extract from speech to the 1992 Conservative Party Conference, in Chitty, C. and Simons, B. (eds), *Education Answers Back: Critical Responses in Government Policy*, Lawrence and Wishart, London.
Miller, B., and Miller, T. (1990), *That's not Fair*, Religious and Moral Education Press, London.
Mullard, C. (1980), *Racism in Society and Schools: History, Policy and Practice*, University of London, Institute of Education, London.
National Curriculum Council (1990), *Curriculum Guidance 3: The Whole Curriculum*, NCC, York, UK.
Rowe, D. and Newton, J. (eds) (1994), *You, Me, Us: Social and Moral Responsibility for Primary Schools*, Home Office, London.
Starkey, H.(ed) (1991), *The Challenge of Human Rights Education*, Cassell, London.
Steiner, M. (1993), Learning from experience: World Studies in the Primary Curriculum, Trentham Books, Stoke-on-Trent, UK.

14 Conclusion

SNEH SHAH

A number of challenges in relation to equality issues in the new millennium were identified in the Introduction. The various authors in this book have presented both philosophical and practical analyses, answering some of the questions posed, and giving an indication of new ways that could lead to a stronger, central context for equality issues in education.

That change is needed despite developments since 1970s is evident. For instance, stereotypes leading to marginalisation, and lack of clarity about the equal opportunities policies of the higher education institutions are amongst the key findings of the recent report in United Kingdom on ethnicity and employment in higher education (Carter et al, 1999). Another example of the nature of change that is needed is typified in the comments by Gathercole (1998). In response to a letter written by Furedi (1998), she finds it unacceptable that (Gathercole, 1998) :

> individuals identified by psychologists as having specific learning difficulties such as dyslexia are either plain lazy or of such low intellectual calibre that we should not encourage their admission to university.

Her conclusion is that the average dyslexic person who is able to get admission to university is likely to have very high levels of intelligence. If such a person is denied a chance to get university education then the next generation is being deprived of brilliant young people.

Defining equality remains a very complex task. Areas normally included are race, culture, gender, special needs, and disability. However, the interconnection between these categories is not fully appreciated. The structure of departments and knowledge is varied within, and across, higher education institutions. There may be examples of a particular focus on special needs in one institution, but that may not necessarily mean all the teaching and learning in that institutions embraces special needs to the same level. It is often the case that it is individual educationalists committed to a particular specialism in equality who have developed its application in the work of the institution.

Each issue is complex in itself, and for policy development and implementation at any level, proper analysis needs to take place. For instance, under-achievement of boys at school can be linked to the lack of male role models at school. This in turn could lead to a drive to recruit more men onto teacher education courses. However, male students are not objects that can be moved like pieces in a board game; they have characteristics, individual and collective, which have resulted from the development of values and beliefs over a long period of time. Having a campaign to have more men on teacher education courses does not automatically mean more men will become qualified teachers, and that in turn will lead to better achievement by male pupils.

Research is thus essential in the untangling of the complexity of such issues. However, bodies funding research need to be aware of the depth of the specific research undertaken. For instance, are the researchers fully aware of the nature of the stereotypic images in their particular areas of research? Have they been able to design their research fully aware of how normal expectations of research, such as sample size and nature of data collection, could in turn produce new stereotypes? Are the funding bodies able and prepared to ensure that the appropriate ethical criteria have been applied? Various authors in this book have commented on the lack of overall progress in an effective implementation of equal opportunities policies in higher education institutions. Such lack of commitment at senior levels could also apply to research and funding bodies.

Employers are often forgotten when equal opportunities policies are monitored. If victims of racism in higher education institutions are able to complete their qualifications, they may need to face and overcome racism when looking for jobs. In a different context, if employers do not use candidates' commitment to equality, then whatever positive developments would have taken place in the education institutions could be negated. Education and training thus needs to be extended to the employers of newly qualified people entering the job market.

Is there a novel way that equality issues can be brought to the centre from the periphery? The term human rights can not only cover strands such as gender, race and special needs, but can be assumed to include any other appropriate aspect of human existence. Because of the general current concern for Universal Declaration of Human Rights and Humans Rights Convention, and the passing of Human Rights Acts in different countries, it may be more readily accepted at senior levels of management. However, if it only applied to individual people's entitlements, then it may help perpetuate many of the disadvantages that it is supposed to rectify. In the past many of the debates about equality led to a focus on specific individuals as the solution. For instance, racial disadvantage was seen to be remedied by increasing the number of minority ethnic people in the relevant contexts. The reasons why the discrimination was able to take place were not often acknowledged to be important. Thus a focus on individual rights may still leave equality on the periphery. If Human Rights are the answer to inequality, then they have to encompass structural changes.

Citizenship can be a very narrow, parochial term but it can also be broad from the point of its meaning and geographical coverage. Equality debates need to acknowledge the inequalities currently existing between different peoples and countries. If approached in a critical way they would become relevant to people in any local geographical area, but embedded in personal and collective challenges for a more just world.

A healthy debate citizenship would underline the value of specific categories in which individuals can be put, but highlight the multiplicity of identities and, therefore, loyalties. In addition, answers to questions like, Who am I, or, Who are You, would control the process whereby individuals are ascribed their identities and loyalties. It is crucial that *everyone* goes through the process of working out their identities. Normally the recognition of multiple identities is linked with minority ethnic people, and the psychological and other problems that ensue. Accepting that *every person* has multiple identities and loyalties achieves two important goals. First of all it does not turn attention to some so-called disadvantaged groups only as everyone is seen to have a disadvantage. Terms such as difference are applied more liberally than as referring to sex and race differences only. Secondly, it brings individuals into a greater dialogue about their own identities and loyalties. If an individual wants to be called deaf, then that is more important than non-deaf people using supposedly less damaging terms such as hearing impaired. Equality thus includes identification as desired by the individuals themselves.

The new term that has recently entered the framework is mainstreaming. This means that equality is built into all systems at all levels, rather than added on. It entails discussion at the planning as well as the implementation stages. Institutions will need to examine their approach to overall planning and working. In some respects this has been the aim of equal opportunity officers. However, mainstreaming should mean that responsibility for effective equal opportunities policies does not just revolve round them. They may be the key person, but the institution at all levels has to understand and undertake its responsibility.

These could include meaningful and innovative developments. Thames Valley University, as reported by Caleb and Gilhooly, was able to make progress partly because the staff were perpetually learning from their experiences, and sharing them. Staff development is often seen simply as individual days/sessions of training. Making staff development an integral, on-going part of the work of the staff can lead to reflective practitioners as often described within the context of school teachers. Research can also be better incorporated in the teaching and learning frameworks.

Perhaps the greatest challenge for the next millennium then is to have policies that are based on the rights and dignity of every human being who is a part of that society. The new millennium should thus be the beginning of a more open, yet more committed approach to equality which does not have boundaries determined by what aspects or issues are included. Instead of market forces, democratic and human rights issues would provide the ethos for the education institutions. It then becomes a real challenge to politicians who have to be prepared to put principles their targets, principles which would upset many of the current power structures.

Bibliography

Carter, J., Fenton, S. and Modood, T. (1999), *Ethnicity and Employment in Higher Education,* Policy Studies Institute, London.

Furedi, F. (1998), 'Examiners Buckle Under an Avalanche of Excuses', letter, in *Times Higher Education Supplement,* 16 October.

Farish, M., McPake, J. and Weiner, G. (1995), *Equal Opportunities in Colleges and Universities: Towards better Practices,* The Society for Research into Higher Education and Open University, Milton Keynes, UK.

Gathercole, S. (1998), letter, in *Times Higher Education Supplement,* 23 October.

Neal, S. (1998), *The Making of Equal Opportunities Policies in Universities,* The Society for Research into Higher Education and Open University, Milton Keynes, UK.

Index

Abdallah-Pretceille, A. 146, 154-6
abuse 14
age 27-28
Agenda 21, 131-141
Ahier, J. 150, 156
Ahsan, M. 39, 45
Alexander, R. 73, 76-77, 87
Americans and Disability Act 98, 104
antiracism 14, 16, 19, 21, 22, 23, 47, 152, 154
Antiracist Teacher Education Network (ARTEN) 48, 60
antisexism 154
Arm, F. 23
Arora, R. 23
assimilation 2, 26
Association of Student Counselling, 112
Association for University and College Counsellors 112
asylum seekers 12
Aune, B. 101

Bahl, K. 9
Baker, C. 122, 129
Baldwin, S. 126, 129
Barot, R. 32
Basit, T. 37, 44
Benjamin, C. 108-109
Bhavnani, R. 27-28, 32
bicultural 122
bilingualism 2, 8, 121-130
Bird, J. 64-65, 70-2
Blackstone, T. 11
Blunkett, D. 90, 101
Boston University 105
Bouvet, D. 122, 129
Bradley, H. 32
British Deaf Association 125, 129
British Sign Language 121-125, 127

Brown, C. 32
Brown, M. 31
Brown, P. 141
Bruntland, G. 132, 141
bullying 14, 20
Burnage Report 56, 60
Bynoe, L. 32

Carter, J. 157, 160
Cassin, R. 146
Centre for Equality 5, 12, 15, 18, 23
Chen, L. 34-35, 44
citizenship 4, 131-141, 146, 159
class 1, 6, 15-16, 18, 20, 27-28, 142, 151
Coard, B. 2, 6, 11
Cole, M. 23, 150, 156
Collins, H. 31
Collison, J. 52, 60
colourblindness 52-53, 55, 58-59
Commission for Racial Equality 3, 5, 7-8, 11, 24-32, 58, 61
Commission on University Career Opportunities 27
Committee of Vice-Chancellors and Principals 12, 27, 31-32
Commonwealth Immigrants Advisory Council 26
Conrad, J. 8, 12
Cooper, J. 29, 32
Council of Europe 143
Cullis-Suzuki, S. 140
cultural diversity 16, 26
culture 158

Department for Education and Employment 4, 125, 129
Department for Education and Science 11
Dearing, R. 90, 92, 104, 109, 151-152
deficit model 2
de-racialized 47-48, 54
Dhamsana, L. 39, 44

Didsbury Study Packs 17, 22
Dijk, T. 4, 11
disability 13-14, 16, 18, 21, 23, 55, 89-110, 121-130,158
Disability Discrimination Act, 3, 90, 91, 96, 101, 104
Disability Statements 95
Disability Student Allowance 91-92, 96-97
Discrimination 17, 21, 28, 30-31
  direct 25-26
  indirect 25-26
DisinHE 101
Drury, B. 38, 44
Dupont-Joshua, A. 116-7, 120
Dyslexia 99, 108, 158

educationally sub-normal (ESN) 2, 12
Education Reform Act 3, 16, 150
Edwards, A. 52, 60
Edwards, S. 88
egalitarianism 1, 5
Egglestone, J. 58, 60
elderly 14
elitism 144
Eleptheriadou, Z. 117, 120
empowerment 12
entitlement 18-19
Equalities Commission 29
Equal Employment Opportunities Commission 104
Equal Opportunities Commission 37, 24-25, 27, 29-32
equal opportunities policy 112-113, 119, 159
ethnicity 27, 31-32
ethnocentrism 18, 33
European Commission 2
European Convention for the Protection of Human Rights and Fundamental freedoms, 144, 146
European Social Fund 3
European Union 152
European Year Against Racism 3, 112
exclusion 7, 11, 13, 18

Farish, M. 160

Farkes, T. 105, 109
feminism 1, 6, 14, 21
Fenton, S. 32, 160
Frankenburg, R. 29, 32
Freire, P. 145, 156
Frith, R. 8, 12
Friends of the Earth, 132
Furedi, F. 157, 160
Further Education Funding Council 27

Gaine, C. 23, 52, 60
Gallaway, C. 124, 129
Gathercole, S. 157, 160
gender 1-2, 5-8, 13-16, 20, 23-32, 47, 73-88, 151, 158-159
George, R. 23
Ghuman, P. 34, 39, 44
Gill, J. 102
Gillborn, D. 15, 20, 23, 47, 51, 60
Gipps, C. 15, 20, 23
Gollnick, D. 51, 60
Grant, C. 61
Gregory, S. 128-129

Hall, J. 125, 129
Halsall, M. 20, 22
Hamilton, J. 12
harassment 27
Harris, m. 123, 129
Hartman, P. 109
Hattersley, R. 14, 23
Haw, K. 36-8, 44
Heads of University Counselling Services 112
Hicks, D. 140-141
Higher Education Funding Council for England 90, 93-96, 101-102
Higher Education Information Trust 101
Higher Education Statistics Agency (HESA), 90, 101
Hill, D. 22, 150, 156
Hillman, J. 90-92, 102
Hillman, M. 138, 141
Hindu 20, 33-44
Hodgkinson, K. 52, 60
homelessness 14, 19
homophobia, 13-14, 150
Honeyford affair 37
Hoskyns, C. 30, 32

Howard, M. 146
human rights 18, 24, 29-30, 32, 142-144, 147, 150-152, 154, 158-160
Human Rights Act 29-30, 158
Human Rights Convention 30, 159
human rights education 145-150, 152-154, 156
Hurst, A. 102
Hutton, W. 16, 23

Illich, I. 15, 23
inclusion 4, 7, 13, 18-19, 22, 101, 121
Inman, S. 141
Institute for Learning and Teaching in Higher Education 102, 108, 109
integration model 2, 26

Jackson, R. 44
Jacobson, J. 37, 44
Jenkins, R. 21
Jewish 21
Jones, C. 66, 70, 72

Kareem, J. 115, 120
Kelly, A. 145, 149, 156
Khalid, R. 41, 45
King, A. 151, 156
Kirchner, A. 126-127, 129
Klein, G. 23
Knight, P. 127, 129
Kohler, G. 145, 156
Kyle, J. 123, 129

Ladd, P. 123, 129
Lang, H. 126, 130
Law, I. 26, 32
lesbian 13-14
Lawson, L. 123, 129
liberalism 7
life chances 14
Loizou, C. 76, 88
Lovelock, J. 137, 141
Lyons, G. 88
Lyseight-Jones, P. 148, 155, 156

MacDonald Inquiry 56
Mackay, R. 52, 61
Macpherson, W. 118, 120
Maguire, M. 66, 70, 72
Mahoney, P. 9, 12
mainstreaming 7, 160-161
Major, J. 143, 156
Manning, J. 91, 102
Marcshark, M. 123, 129
Marion, L. 34-35, 44
Mason, M. 23
McDermott, M. 39, 44
McPake, J. 160
Meadows, D. 141
melting pot 26
Milani, A. 98, 102
Miller, B. 147, 156
Miller, T. 147, 156
Millett, A. 88, 74
Mitchell, P. 151, 156
Modood, T. 34, 44, 160
morality 146-147
Mullard, C. 143, 156
multiculturalism 14, 19-20, 23, 44, 47, 49-50, 56, 152
Muslim, 33-44

Naipaul, V. 37, 44
NASFIYAT International Therapy Centre 115
National Association of Head Teachers (NAHT), 73-74, 88
National Bureau for Students with Disabilities 90
National Committee of Inquiry into Higher Education, 90-91
National Committee for Commonwealth Immigrants 25
National Curriculum 6, 13, 17-18, 23, 25, 47, 143, 150
National Curriculum Council 141, 149, 157
National Disability Council 3
Neal, S. 160
Nesbitt, E. 45
Newton, J. 146, 157
Nightingale, P. 8, 12
Non-Governmental organisation (NGO) 132

Nye, M. 78, 88

O'Hanlon, C. 91, 102
Okorocha, E. 120
O'Neil, M. 8, 12
Orr, D. 137, 141
Ouseley, H. 9
Owen, D. 32
Oxfam 132

Parekh, B. 11
Parker-Jenkins, M. 37, 38, 44
Patten, J. 75
Pepperell, S. 78, 88
permeation 48-49, 59
Petrie, H. 102
Philips, R. 4
Phippen, M. 112, 119-120
Pickersgill, M. 126-129
Plowden, B. 137, 141
pluralistic model 2
Potts, P. 23
poverty 14-15, 20
Powers, S. 125, 130
Powney, J. 12
Protection from Harassment Act 3

quality 8, 12
Quarrie, J. 132-133, 141

race 1, 5, 6, 7, 16, 18, 24-32, 47-49, 52-53, 57, 142, 151, 158
race relations 2, 12
Race Relations Act 1, 3, 26, 30.
Race Relations Board 26
Race Relations Commission 26
racial disadvantage 23
racial discrimination 6, 31
racial justice, 13
racial prejudice 20
racism 3, 19, 20, 23, 31-32, 144-145, 150, 153, 159
Rampton report, 2, 4
Rana, R. 120
Reddall, D. 107, 109
refugees, 12, 152
Rehabilitation Act 104
Richard, B. 129
Reiser, R., 23

Riley, K., 23
Roberts, H. 23
Robertson, D. 90-92, 102
Roots to the Future Project 31
Ross, A. 156
Rowe, D. 146, 156

Sanders, P.,12
Schumacher, E. 136, 141
School Curriculum and Assessment Authority, 3-4, 12, 141
Scoffham, S. 141
Segal Quince Wickstead 102
Selman, P. 135-6
sex discrimination, 31
sex equality 2, 73-88
Sex Discrimination Act,1, 3, 25
Sexism 21-2, 31, 144-145, 150
sexuality,16-17, 142, 151
Section 11 2, 4
Shalet, R. 106-107, 109
Shan, S. 22, 151, 156
Shaw, J. 102
Shephard, G. 137, 146
Shiner, M. 34, 144
Siann, G. 42, 45
sign language 125
Sikhs 20, 33-44
Singh, G., 23
Siraj-Blatchford, I. 58, 60, 63, 72
SKILL 90, 94
Skinner, G. 45
Smedley, S. 78, 88
Smith, A. 109
Smith, D. 15, 23
Smith, E. 120
Smith, S. 109
social change 31
social justice 5-6
social policy 32
Southall Black Sisters 116
Sparkes, A. 52, 61
special needs 2, 5, 6, 7, 151, 158-159
Spence, S. 32
Starkey, H. 143, 146, 156
Steiner, M. 141, 147, 156
Stephen Lawrence Inquiry 118
stereotypes 10, 17, 21, 26, 28, 34, 44, 53, 88, 144, 159

Sternberg, R. 107-108
Stimson, M. 126, 130
subversion 18
Swann Report 4, 41, 48

Tate, N. 3-4
Teacher Training Agency 4, 58, 61, 73-74, 84-85, 88, 109
Thames Valley University 111-120, 161
tokenistic approach 2
Tomlinson, S. 41, 45
Troyna, B. 23
Taylor, P. 42, 45

unemployment 20
Universal Declaration of Human Rights 143-144, 152, 158
Universities Central Admissions Service 91
Universities Central Council for Admissions 42
University of East London 91-97
University of Georgia 98, 102
University of North Dakota 98, 102

Verma, G. 38, 40, 45, 72
victimisation 26
Visible Women Project 28, 31

Wade, R. 136, 141
Wail, P. 110
Walkling, J. 120
Warnock Report 2
Watson, B. 66, 70, 72
Weiner, G. 12, 161
Westman, J. 110
Wigley, J. 23
Williams, J. 23
Woll, B. 123-124, 129
Wood, K. 140-141
Woodrow, D. 35, 45
World Education Fellowship 141
World Summit 131-133, 141

xenophobia 153

Yu, P. 29, 32

Zec, P. 45